Love, Death, and Freedom herself

By
CHARLIE
ARLEY

Love, Death, and Freedom herself

Print ISBN 13: 979-8-9889066-0-5
eBook ISBN 13: 979-8-9889066-1-2
Library of Congress Control Number: 2023914710

Published by Charlie Monroe
Written and Created by Charlie Arley
Director of Art Charlie Arley
Cover illustration by Jibrahim
Internal illustrations by Yana Nunes
Photograph by Scott Womack

ATTENTION: SCHOOLS AND BUSINESSES
Charlie Arley's books are available at quantity
discounts with bulk purchase for educational,
business, or sales promotional use. For information,
please e-mail the Charlie Monroe Publishing Sales Department:
CharlieMonroeSales@gmail.com

MUSIC PRODUCERS/MUSICIANS CONTACT ME***
Contact @ Back of book.

For the curious people. & the teachers...

Table of Contents

100 select poems. Read in order on initial read through.

Love—

Death—

Freedom herself—

Presenting

Love, Death, and
Freedom herself

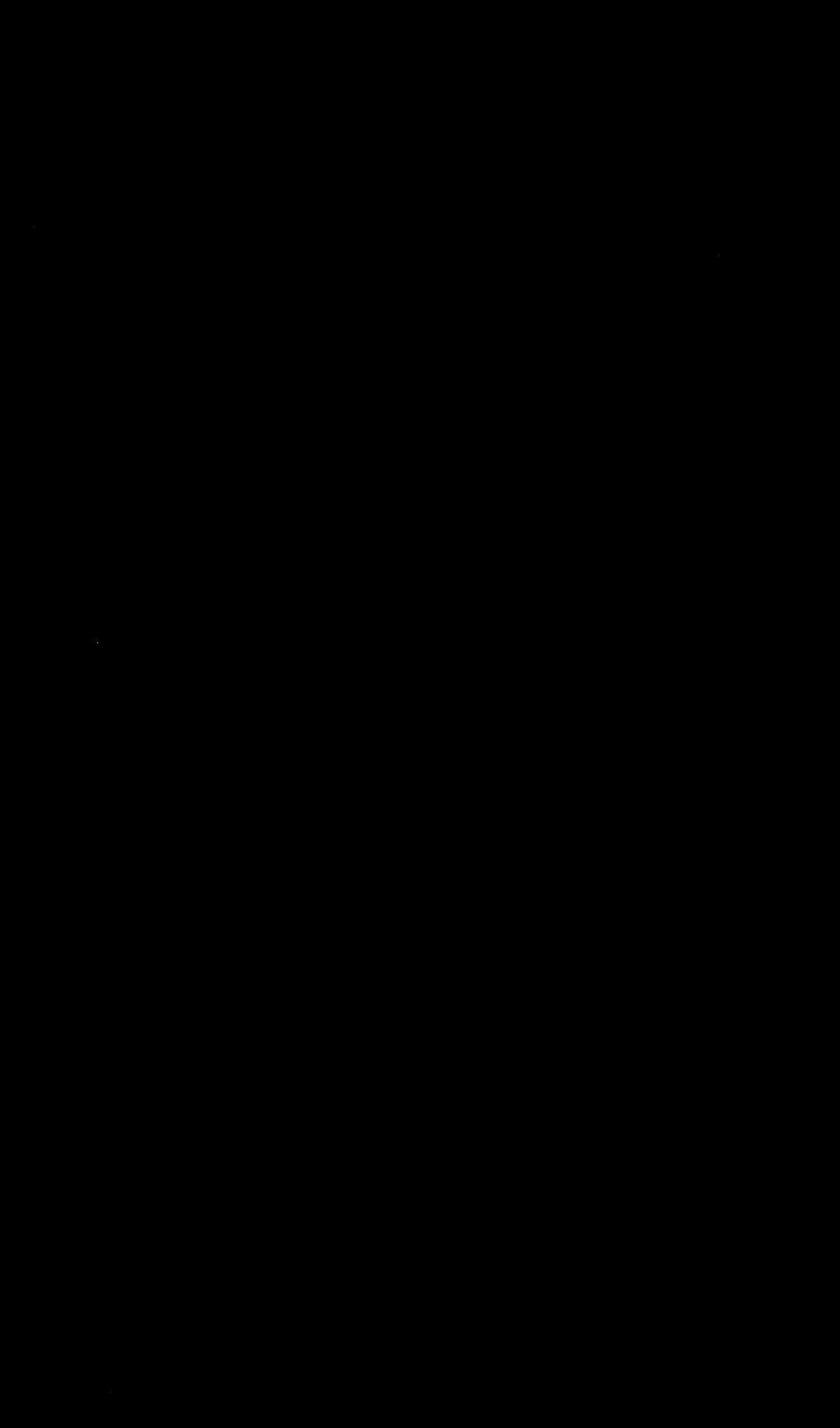

love

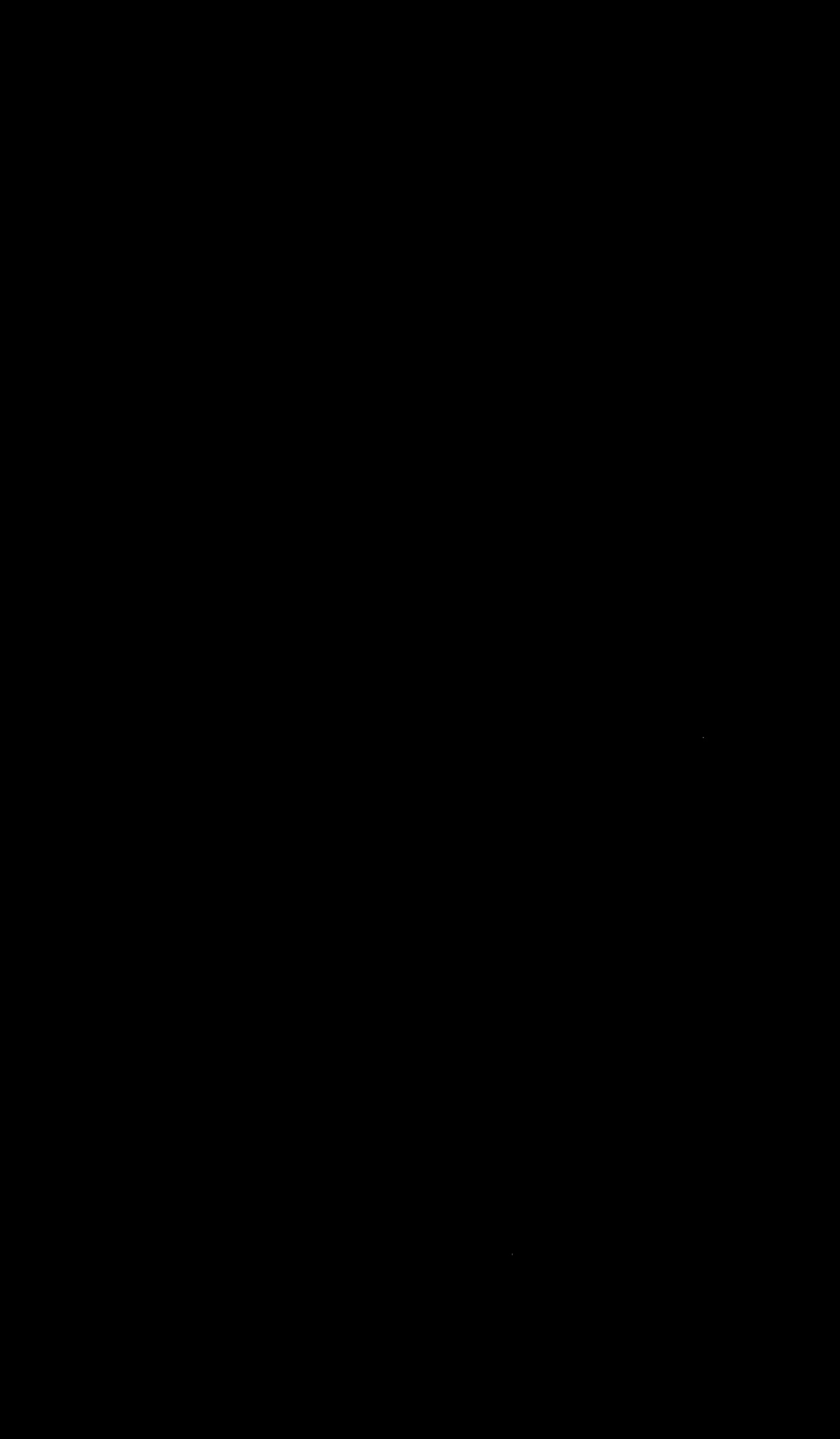

Purpose

11/1/22

Fill my heart with tranquility and hold it to high standards.

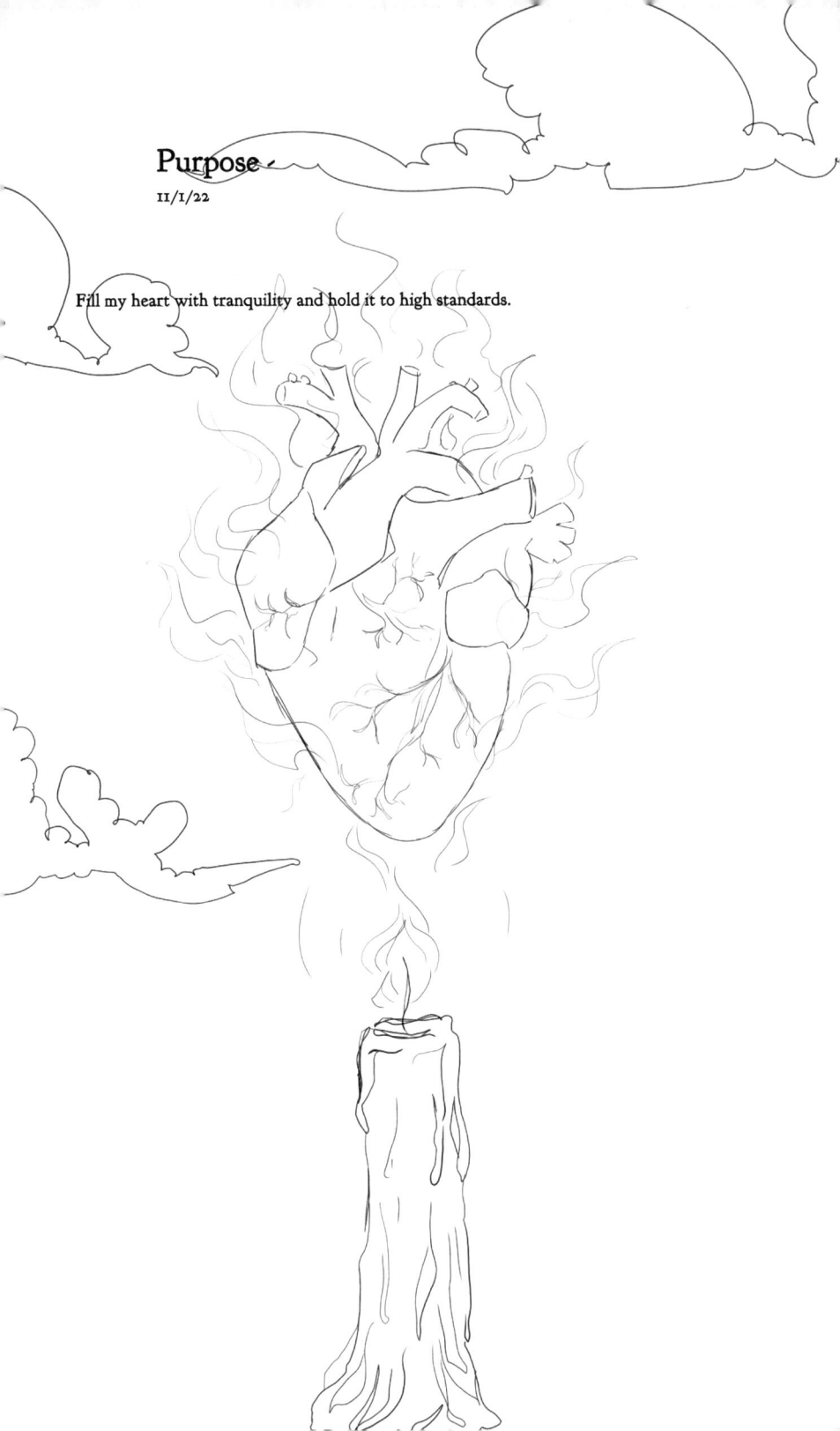

In Bloom, ⸌

3/5/23

A child
solemnly crouched in a sandbox—
His mind, predisposed to mutation—

Like a blossoming rose that flows in the wind,
he collects whatever he may come across.

He's stuck in cotton-brained infancy until tomorrow,
But tomorrow never comes, does it—
Always escaping to the next day.

Expansion and pain happens,
Rebirth and transmogrification—

Change is time's relentless pet—

Staged towels ⸻

10/4/22

Lives led by luxury lead to less.
Wives freed by jewelry breed distress.
Knives that bleed foolery supersede a mess.
What do you need–?
Now that's a question to impress...

Gorgeous Girl eager to undress—
    —Laughs that grow like a weed
—Paths that lead to happiness,
I can remember times in my life that have been a mess—
Now I smile and let my fears wash and digress.

Crows chirping soothes the nerves especially at dawn.
I, used to feel dour, now, I, wake with a smile and a yawn.
Not even she can tell you what my rich life has been on—

But as time matures and the days grow richer
    It'll become increasingly more difficult to show them my picture.

Dreams of her ⸗
3/23/23

Wet wood brings such sweet scents.
Trees as tall as buildings rashed with green,
Moss-corroded rocks, and lustrous flowers give dashes of contrast to the color of fog.
Cackling rain conquers the space beneath the clouds.
Me and my darling lay in silk grass, our bodies wisped and cradled like statues laid in
cotton.
cuddled up.

My darling is love.

Some days this bubbled emotion escapes me.

Fear can drive love away, while pensive being can lead to romanticized solitude.

There are countless forms of love, and each can be as dynamic of an essence as any other.
But some just get you...
When you desire to control and regulate how love is presented and at what time,
you are forgetting the supple, the sweet,
how awesome a treat,
love's so bizarre and timeless,
watch it hang by its feet.

—When love goes away and upside down,
it is not entirely your fault...
Just understand that as you develop,
there are some learning curves that you must vault.

—at the end of the day,
Love does not need to stay.

I'll tell you what,
You're capable of endless love.
Look at the mirror, the individual whomst understands your situation best,
Believe me that being in the reflection pool, grows unlike the rest.

Love works in mysterious ways with ambiguity—
See it in the lined dance of the ants,

See it in the aquatic underbellies of the arctic.
Go outside, gaze upon the night sky.

My god, there's love right there.

Look at the line dance of the cosmos.
Omnipotent. Love.

Sidereal love ⸝

6/19/23

Beneath the vast radiant starscape—
I feel as though I can finally breathe.
No longer being choked by the claustrophobic clouds of the Pacific Northwest,
I can release and look outwards for a moment.

I lay rest, alone in the darkness with nothing but crickets and the wind's sweet whistle.
The smell of kicked dirt finds shelter in my nose,
Nothing can turn my focus away from the sprinkled celestial gleam overhead.

A cosmic line dance,
A ghastly spectacle presented to my yearning eyes.

Sitting on my now cold, smooth stone blanket, I feel soothed...
Surrounded by nothing but empty space.
—There's room for remembrance.

This sort of freedom is rooted in solitude,
It's okay to disappear when you require refocus.
Disappear and face your frontier of fear,
Blossom with your lotus of love.
The end is close, the end is near.

Shhh...
Listen.   The polka dots speak.

"True beauty such as this, surrounds you in moments you searched for nothing but your soul.
Cherish the now my child, for it's you who imbues you whole.

Look ahead my child,
That bright star there points you towards the north most pole.
That spot may or may not be your largest true goal."

Breathe, embrace moments as they speak—
Allow as paroxysms of calm wash away identity,
Ease into unease—

then all that remains is,
flesh and celestial illumination—

A natural serenade ⁓

7/7/23

The gentle rustling of leaves,
The rough skin,
The quiet whispers of the wood.
How amazing it is that I can symbiotically exist with this species,
An overflow of wisdom that you can taste.
Sedentary, yet ever expanding.
I breathe out for it to breathe in,

I ask it,
"What is life like, free from laws?"

It responds with astute poise and an ever-calming silence.
I'm communicated with through the world of awe.

My intuition sings and gives life to dancing words inside my head,
These words burn bright, before forgotten and dead—
"Hush now my child, we live in the same world, where mountainous peaks soar, and
there's pearlescent beauty on the ocean floor.

These laws exist, and we both abide,
For it is from nature's laws that we cannot hide.

Although I live without eyes,
A life lived free from corrupted lies.
And while I have never lived with fear,
I understand that my time is ever near.

Don't be human and fret on death,
When you can embrace nature and take a deep breath."

Aphelion desires ✑

5/5/22

Sunshine daydream—
This interaction has an obviously common theme.
A theme of the cold inviting perfume you wear,
The scent of your unwashed, glossed hair,
The soft satin of your pink underwear.

These evokers have visceral effects.
Giving birth to a reckless deal;
A deal meant to tether our likeness—
or design us as intimate strangers,
Through the universal medium of raw impact love.

Just somebody that I know ✑

12/11/22

Twisted turnips turn me tipsy—
I love when she bites, when she nips me,
I can't get enough of her hips, she...
Needs a gentle touch and kind words.

Hot toasted sincerity, with little impurity.

What's impossible?
I forgot—
The world keeps spinning—
There's no stopping curiosity—

Rose skin ✎

6/12/23

Rose skin,
taste of chocolate.

Trust me,
I am good for you sweetheart.

I'm glad you are happy.

What's a lover? ✔

11/25/22

A lover, the iris of an eye,
Where passion blooms and fears go awry.

love letter ⸌

12/14/22

I'm just a wild child,
Finding my desire.
I will never tire enough to retire and hang up.
Show me the bashful, the dreadful, the beauty.
Happiness cannot exist without suffering.
Things die, the matter isn't voided,
the matter returns to its environment,
and life returns.

If you never got to struggle,
you'd never witness rebirth.

Tell me! Please do share.
Share with me what's under there!
My dear, allow me a peek inside your mind,
I promise to not judge the horrors I may find.
This pink biomass resting within your skull's bone cradle,
It produces your one-of-a-kind experience, peculiar and rich.
Which seems to me babe,
in the grand scheme of my all, not to be dull.

...

I am captivated by love and will let my body follow,
Being guided towards gentle rest and sweet caress.

I know I'll be alright even through my sharp and fall,
as I do claim to be human and resilient after all...

Sweetheart,
The internal love I feel, will always belong to me,
Nothing can strip me of it,
regardless of situation.

But,

I'd like to share it with you.

...

I found green jasper on the beach today after a catacombed tunnel—
It reminded me of a lover's touch.

Even as I ask for it all,
I need for you to understand that, for what I offer,
everything isn't much.

The feeling of discourse I get when I lose sight of the real, is something of mine that lacks appeal.

I want to love, provide and nourish a soul,
I want to be somebodies, most fun, flourishing goal,
Believe me, I'm worthwhile, I'm not common coal.

Til' now and forever, I'll have my own set of faults,
My attention will be required. But
do understand,
Solving these faults is not the role of my lover.
Protect my spirit.

The ocean waves' painless thrash,
causes me to forget malice.

I know that love is to be fostered, and
that indecision would be its decay.

Love the beauty, will seek me and cherish my soul, for I am a kind heart.
I seek to leave positive impacts and flush myself with art.

To whomever possesses my love,
If I had fevered freedom I'd get in a car,
drive to a bay in which we would meet.
A hug and a kiss is how we would greet,
smiles would flutter and cheek lines would print,
I will never get old of your voice.
It is not trash nor
Is it lint.

You are a treasure I will not forget.
My love is rash and wild,
...you want it.

Times shifting tapestry ✓

10/18/22

Salt used to trade its weight in gold,
Now look at what we'd rather hold.

When determining the value of anything,
Ask yourself what your larger goals are.
And what fortune means to you,

Richness.
Health,
Wealth,
& Community.

She prompted me with a beguiling dance,
And gave a hot whisper into my ear,
"Let's see the edge of morning tomorrow,"
The vision of what could be,
was sharper than any image.

She continued,
"We can run drills— we can play scrimmage..."

Fruitful are those eyes.
Irresistible are her thighs.
Minds melt together.
I'm eager.
I'm moved.
To me, she is valuable,

A voice materialized, sophisticated in its speech.
Explained that what's valuable is different to each,

"This is precious experience that you wield,
experience it fully and cherish what's revealed.

These moments won't last forever and upon first glance,

that may seem bad, but hear me out, give me a chance.

Remember in history, salt was worth more than gold,
and as your life moves, new experiences you will hold.

This wishful relation it may last,
but if it crumbles don't linger too long on the past.

For life will transition and new things will be bold,
As it is, remember, today's salt may be tomorrow's gold."

With this realization that rings within my ear,
I know that 'loss' should not be what I fear.
The brine of tears throughout the years,
Will show me how ignorant I was to hold those fears.

For time shall churn, and I will learn,
That as a kingdom receives its salt,
it is gold that in time, this kingdom will exalt.

But the time is now so I shall embrace,
"Regress my darling", darl
Sightless seeing.
Effortless being.

Can I have a smile and a kiss.
Thank you, bite—

Reflection glass ✓

6/5/21

I'd no idea what could change,
I'd like to see a, change,
Free a thought or two—
What to do, rearrange
And interchange my thoughts.

Take a look inside my mind,
you'll be surprised as to what you might find.
Do you speak to art, or does it speak to you?
Sometimes we may find ourselves trapped.
Trapped between who we are and all that we want to be.
Sometimes all we crave to be is free.
And occasionally all we need,
is to sit with another beneath a shaded tree.

Growth is an interesting creature.
Sometimes we need another to be our teacher.
Sometimes we need to reconnect to childish love and play.

Tell me now, are you a moonchild?
Does sunlight dance upon your hair?
Are you willing to fit me into the things that hold your care?
Care will be my epitaph.
Drawn as a swirl—

I believe in—
Words and values,
People and places,
Feelings and faces.

Within me, there lies a sweet desire.
I'd like a face to see—
My ups and downs.
I want to understand
someone's ups and downs,
Their smiles and frowns.
Love's not a game of crowns

power isn't the objective.

I can be outspoken, I can be quiet, I will listen, I can help.
What about you?
Are you a giver or a taker?
Real or a faker?
A destroyer or a maker?

...

Why does life pause under the stars,
Out here on the perimeter we are free children.
There is slow progress under these stars.
Wild child, care not what others think—
Your mindset is something that you should occasionally rethink.

We need not a dim candle to see,
For when I speak to the breeze—
It seems to carry my words free.

Maybe I might ⸌

10/3/21

Maybe I will, maybe I won't.

But you don't have to give me my decision.
It comes naturally, it comes after me.

Everything, is a play, a grand play,
put on by the universe, okay? Alright.
For no other reason, but to experience itself,
And an infinite night.

On this stage that we live in,
our universe perceiving.
Remember one thing.

Everything, it matters, but nothing's a big deal.

Everything is matter,
but what's the big deal?

Perhaps the biggest deal is just, how you feel.
I'm not searching for the best play, just a human one.
I'm not looking for recognition,
just to share.
I'm not hoping for money, just a little bitty taste of freedom.

Watch the play, play.

I am human,
high highs, low lows
I I go go,
wherever I will.
Strange folks, strange jokes,
Strange times, strange wines.

Love, hope or death.

Mysterious death.

Come show me your shelter lady mortality.
Show me, who you are.
Eventually, I'd love to meet.

But I'd like to warn you,

I'm just another passing.
I am passing,
Passing through the days.
Playing through my plays.
Weeks, months, years
watch as time boils your fears.

Through you, lady mortality.
Through you, lady mortality.

You'll just have to see.

It'll be grand in whatever fashion it may be.
Whatever happens is true reality—
actually, it's just part of my discovery.

happened, happening and happens all at once.
Trust was scarce, while I was amongst;
a lot of people,

that I've known,

Love, sex, money.
Life, strangers, honey.

Pleasurable trauma,
PTSD,
can I be me?

Find hope, in whatever's around.

look at your fellow humans and celebrate.
lust for life, joy and pain, sun and rain,
cold months,
hot hours,
Hotter showers.
freeeeee to think...

To explore with love ⸌

5/26/22

I dreamt a drowsy daydream of rose-orange sand, washed by wine-colored sky.
A promontory filled with beautiful asphalt, crystal boulevards never to be crossed.

Constructed with happiness—
O happiness, O harmony, O hedonism!

Rich gardens illuminated her noisy dress.
Luminous flowers found cursing hearts.
Ruby red lips and the perfume of a polar sun.
Red meat and red velvet.
O happiness, O harmony, O hedonism.

hair and eyes—
The voice of a woman.
As blazing as the depths of the volcanoes! And the arctic grottoes!
O happiness, O harmony, O hedonism!

This golden dawn was flooded with warm breeze,
And tremendous views of coastal dunes.

O happiness, O harmony, O hedonism!

Why the painter paints. ⌐

why does the painter paint?
Outside of external incentives that is.
Such as money, influence, social status, etcetera, you get the point.

Perhaps you lean towards psychological reasoning.
Seeking insight on the painter's cognitive conditioning. To deduce,
'The painter's inclination to paint is simple, predictable, purely a function of biological
constraint.
It's formulaic, driven by background math.
Reward mechanisms, stimuli— it's all in the painter's neural wiring.

It seems,
Sensations the painter perceives artistic,
grant their brain joyful jolts.

Allow me to experiment:

'3/23/23'.   *bzzzzzttt,*

"Wow, I liked that."

'6/26/23'.   *bzzzzztttt,*

"Wow, I liked that."

'12/12/22'.   *bzzzzztttt,*

"Wow, I liked that."

Could be, could be. We
definitively, try to see, our reality, objectively, and scientifically.
But,
perhaps the true reason as to why the painter paints
lays beyond that understanding—
What we call 'natural order'.

Now,
You could argue that a painter paints for the sake of probability.

But...
Is it truly just math? The brush strokes of Van Gogh?
Could it be purely material? Or are there degrees of abstractions at play?

I think.

In an attempt to understand my acquaintance with beauty.
In the pursuit of discovery. I'll explore my skepticism.
Do we comprehend beauty's influence within the will of this reality?

I think not.

A hidden dance camouflaged by veil.
Beauty influences movement within the tangible.
It operates through means and realities that, to us, are intangible.
As an abstract exists, I believe the physical bear's reaction.
Perhaps beauty has sway in the movement of energy...
To determine if this guess has scientific bearing, seems to me, to be
out of this eras' grasp.

...

Deduce.

The 'creation' of the universe,
The Big Bang— matters beginning.
Has inherent beauty.
An event too bizarre to be fictitious,
the dawn of movement.

Now, follow along...
The existence of atoms is dependent on the actuality of matter, and,
The actuality of matter is dependent on the existence of atoms.
One cannot exist without the other.

That being said. I grow conscious of beauty's inherence within creation.
This inherence seemingly makes our realities existence impossible without the presence of
beauty.
Reality cannot exist without beauty, because reality is inherently beautiful.

Beauty's presence lays foundation to our universe's origin, seemingly
being a requirement to have capacity for anything.

Thus, I infer that without beauty itself, the very fabric of our reality would cease.
Just as creation requires atoms, to be.

...

I sit here, tasting the beauty of the abstract.
I believe I understand... that I don't understand.
Although, after all my inspection,
I do believe I've figured out why the painter paints.

the painter paints,
because beauty is.
If,
beauty isn't, then,
a painter wasn't.

The painter paints to fulfill requirement,
enabling the presence of beauty.
The painter cannot allow for beauty's death,
because, without beauty.
The painter is not.

...

What is beauty?
Its scope is unknown.

Why is it to be seeked?
Our life,
cannot 'be'
without it.

why, oh sailor why? ✓

5/2/23

ohhh, sailor do you know,
at the seashore watermelon grow.
If you stop and close your eyes,
tasteful beauty you may find.

Reflective interpretations ⸝

8/24/21

I'm elusive and evasive,
I disappear and reappear,
I'm a contradiction filled with cognitive dissonance.
I'm a figment of someone's imagination.
I don't mind going unseen and lingering in the shadows—

What am I?
A ghost? A dream? A thought?
Time? A shadow? An enigma?
Myself?

Could be.

But I suppose that is for you to decide.
Allow your intuition to guide you,
while reading, while experiencing, while existing.
Finding your authentic truth.

Your experience doesn't need to fit into any single "universal answer".
When you search for yourself, don't allow your own mind to hide you.
Listen to yourself, and allow self-love to guide you—

All these writings are, are prompts.
Find lessons that are true to your reality.
Interpret your perception.
& never stop loving your moral truth—

Suspect ⸌

12/24/21

I don't know who the suspect is, but I suspect it's someone suspected, probably the most suspicious.

Ohhh, to know the golden ingredient... ✓

1/2/23

Seek out the discomfort, seek out the pain,
find things that push you,
and do not hide from the rain.

Embrace uncertainty and follow your passions relentlessly.
Pay attention, be keen.
Embrace life's simple punities and keep it pushing—
Do not let discontent be seen.

...

If you push for betterment,
Life shall be bountiful and great.
A content, kind existence without hate
is what you shall create.

I've seen times of evil and vapid toxicity.
These times of rot instilled a rare gratitude, that only a personal hell could produce.

Do not forget your kind words,
thank you and please, remember to compliment and
playfully tease.
For when you're a genuine person, others' angst may release.

I strive to wander Earth, kindly ambitious,
reaping life's little moments.

To achieve such, I shall often ponder on the dead.
So as to instill the idea that,

'When I stop to rest my head, for the last time.
—I hope to hold not an ounce of hate.
For it's a kind future that I strive to create.
And I know all too well that it is never too late,
Unless my fleshly world were to—
disintegrate.'

Life's proctoration ⸍
1/2/23

At the first croak of dawn,
I sit here and wipe the cold from my eyes as I yawn.
There've been times I've sat as a pawn,
a unit that can be easily replaced when gone.

Now I feel as though I sit as something greater,
as I breathe with mindful rest.
I've found a peaceful truth:
Life is my proctor, and pain is my test.

I have grown into the best version of myself that I've known.
So...
it's in my best interest to
keep pursuing the golden inquisition:
How can kindness be shown?

Faith ✓

11/13/22

We must practice patience as we wait for purpose,
Prepare your strength and discipline, for,
there will be a time soon in which you must execute.

Airport blues in March ⸱
3/23/23

Tiles roared blue as I walked through,
Doubtless-minded people hurried around my soul.

A businessman discontent with his shortcoming— shrugs
as to not allow himself the disrespect—
—he missed his attempt to score on an idle garbage can.

Children prancing, avoiding the green tiles,
stepping on my delicate blue.
Oh, will there be greatness!
oh, will there be hue!

Music allows time for reminder.
Reminding my mind that I'll find something that's worth my time;
such as reminders.

Overhearing's of a premature labor: 2 months early spells disaster. Tragedy can be all-
encompassing in this world. But to endure is the human condition. And to succeed is a
given if you trust your mind's kindness and intuition.
Hard work is the key.

Children holding safe hands.
Witnesses to airport stimulation, carrying wide eyes.
Nothing to dim their vision, it's a part of their condition. Curiosity.

Wheelchaired members of our human race that hold sympathetic growls within their
eyes.
I wonder how many children it took to sew the good vibes shirt.

I know that in my heart, after my life concludes,
the conscious dialogue that shall leave my cold vessel
shall find itself wrapped in the beauty of the universe's mystery.
As each day passes,
as I stumble towards death,
ohhh each day I clumsily walk towards death,
Ohhh each day that's written, rumbling towards death,
They write like history.

Seeing angels ˏ

4/11/23

Some nights as I sit and sigh,
I see my moon dressed in a halo—
Oh, how beautiful a nimbus can be.

The thought of its photons racing to give me their presence—
Gives me a sense of callous peace, helping me release
My unintended detrimental dreams— through
Harmonious acceptance—

...I've no other option.

...

Harmony:
Hold me however you'd like.

Hold me in the woolly brain of your interest.
Hold me in the camouflage of your hate.

Harmony:
Show me whatever you'd like.

Show me the whimsical nuance associated with your charm.
Show me the painful dissolve tied to your harm.

...

Like life, like sentences,
Like the photons bouncing off my eyes, granting me vision of something beyond.
Everything visits, for only but a period.

I've been told a secret. Do you want to hold it? To hear it?
Oh, sweet child, forever yearning,
Your days on Earth are—
ever burning.

Keep yourself whole, and fill your role—

Do what you can.
And when the unexpected happens,
that you didn't see coming, that doesn't fit the plan.
Please understand,

Desire's avoidance is meant to be grand—
That is why we must rest our heads in the sand.
For only but a period, for then we must look.

Because...
If you wait too long,
When your head pops from the ground and you see your reflection through another's
perception.
You'll see the halo that you hold—
That is when you'll say something, so very bold.
"Oh dear, my time now,
it's old."

Transform and accept

1/7/23

This is the day of diabolical deviation—
This is the song of the fruited bird—
This is the freedom of an unsung hero—

To become what you must become, you must become aware of what you must become.

Something bad happened...
Maybe it's a blessing.

The undesired edge of morning—
With seven sweet seasons of countless sweet caressing having gone by...
The cat's now on its eighth life.

Today has been another day you live in a blessing.
Peek inside your mind,
You'll be surprised as to what you may find—
Some things are so bright, you might go blind.

I'll tell you this much,
of something I'm quite fairly sure;
Never stop trying to be kind...
Because an uncaring life
is a life lived poor.

Love mantra, ✓

7/17/23

Dear—,
I love you—

death

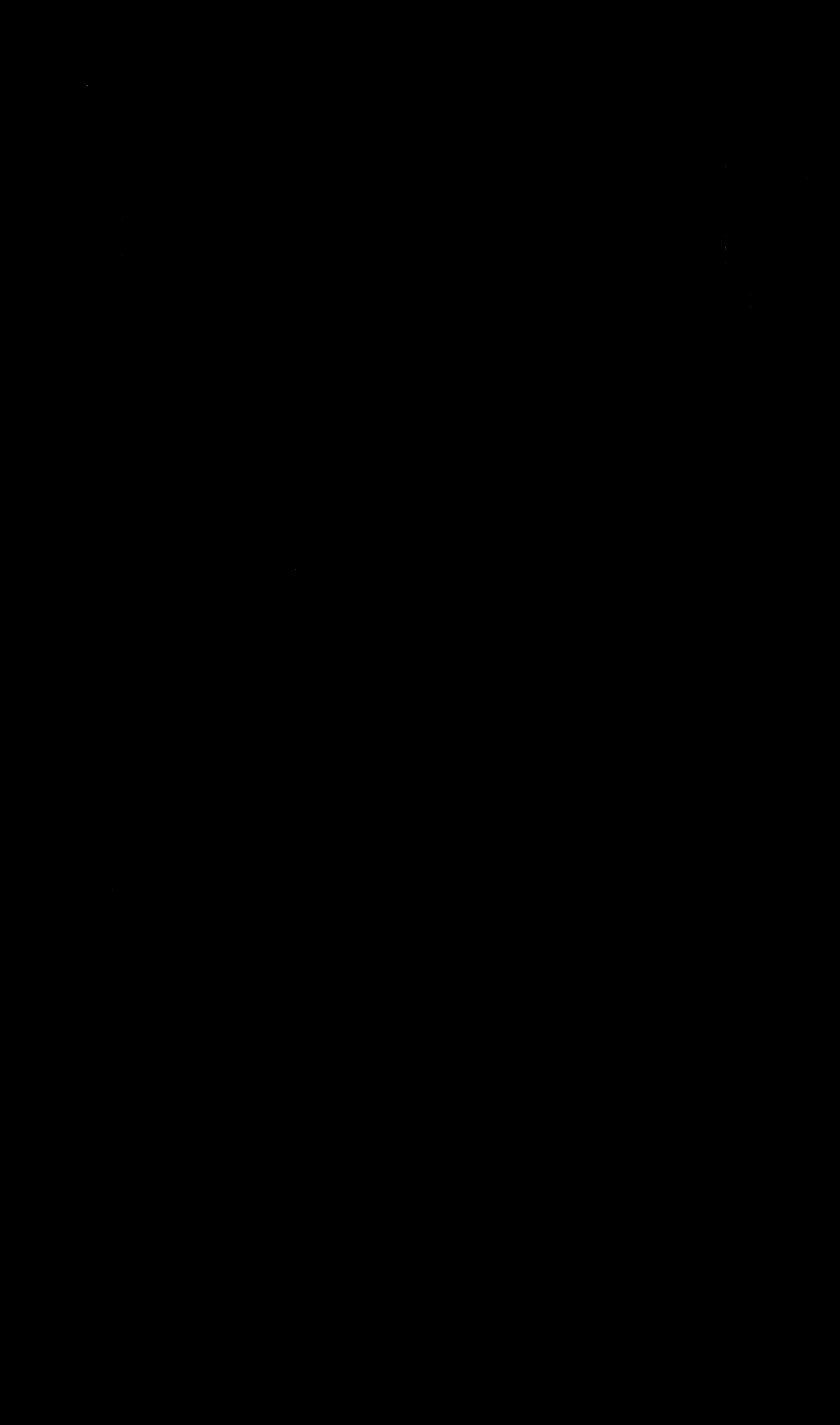

Dear death, ⸜

9/24/21

Dear death, I must confess—
My life's been thrown around and I've made a mess.
What could you do to grant me peace?
Well for starters, I'd like to sit down with you to feast, Watermelon, honeydew and
stringed meat,
So many things to talk over and beat.

I'd like to find a girl in a dress,
Hair unkempt, a mess,
Dress our characters—
Strung in silk—

A good-time, grand-enough to unhang the hung.
Maybe I should've sung her a song, ahhh...
Who cares, whatever...

I'd rather live life as 'me', compared to living life as a pretender, because,
If I was a created creature bound to be found out,
I'd have to surrender.

My life like paper, has been folded,
So, I ask of you,
Great lord, great death—
To give me an experience worth the extra breath...

Laqueum ✒

5/8/23

When you die,
The storms of pathos will laugh with joy, as you
find your final destination to be brilliantly coy.
Compellingly showing how little troubling oneself helped—

Take charge of your life's prerogative through visions of fate.
Embrace the feeling that one day you'll be late.
Accompany death on her horses' laden saddle,
your flesh needn't be rotten to achieve said battle.

"Oh foolish brain, you scream what's false,
Always about such simple things,
That make me simple, like a screw.
For once, I'll tell you now what's true!

Once I tame your booming voice,
I'll get to pick 'bouts what I care,
I won't fall victim to your snare.
I'll have choice."

This is when you sit death on your lap,
Whisper sweet nothings 'til she's off to nap.
Then you shall pick up her scythe,
and lick the blade sharper than any knife.

When you get a taste for what's to come,
the grasp of cruel bindings will be numb.
It is then that you will soar above,
uncertain findings that to her, are dumb.

Preach about pain to teach about pain. ✔

The demons are screaming.
I'm at the bay of the ocean,
Swinging in my sweet rocky cradle,
As high tide approaches—
The space between, me and my water—
encroaches.
—I can almost reach out like a needy baby and finally grasp what barrier has been
between me and myself.

Soon I will be swallowed,
And this gunk in my soul will be hollowed.

I brace for the presence of a new god and whisper callously into the wind,
as the—
distant voices approach.
"Somebody needs a gentler and more whimsical soul."
I'm a melting pot, a bowl full of intensity.
Ready to reveal obvious truths:

'A hat my dear is something that's worn,
Your birth year my dear is the year you were born.'

Fill my soul with tranquility and hold me to high standards.
Don't allow the evils of the world to conquer another soul.
Life is within your control,
Evil is necessary for your maturement,
Trees grow crooked sometimes,
But that is to achieve a larger goal,
To capture sunlight.

Believe me, as high tide approached, it tried to kiss me.
My original spot may have had distance and comfort.
But as time played its harmonious tune,
less than a foot was left between my flesh and the furthest reach of the ocean,
the unknown,
the demons roared in my ears certainly, barked even—
But there I sat,
Immaculately embracing, immovable.

Unable to be manipulated by my demons, my body was torn into pieces.
My conscious mind raced out the door and let in spirits—As they danced in my head

My body tingled.
Pulled towards the moon I was—
I am what I does.

Don't let the voices of the sheep tell you where to go,
And when to go.
Everyone is calling it a day at the beach and heading in.

I'm just sitting here considering my day a win,
Ready to face the cold.
I've learned to seek discomfort.
I certainly won't get penetrated, let alone bleed.

In life I desire a plot of grass to plant my seed, so an apple tree can grow and bear me fruit.
Certainly, life can provide,
As long as you embrace life's turns and twists,
And develop competence as trouble persists.

As I sit and refind my mind
I fathom the peaceful places that I may find.
Within my life on planet Earth
Some greatness will be the reward of rebirth.

This cold is a demon I love to taste,
Because when it comes knocking, I slam the door in its face.
Tell it, 'I'm stronger' than what it can do,
This color of blue isn't an overwhelming hue.

Can't you see I'm my own friend.
I'll be with him till the day that I end.
I've embraced my own company
and will help him progress,
For he dreams of freedom, and to help when there's a mess.

Freaks freaks and pagodas,
I am a lovely dancing freak,
Roaming mindfully across my planet.
I've known many freaks, even some as tastefully sour as pomegranate.

As

The

Cold
Returns to the forefront of his mind,

He learns a special gift—

Between his soul and his mind there is a rift,
It ripped at birth and to sew it together is his mission on earth.

Cobbled dungeness rocks lay beneath his feet.
These rocks are cold, trying to take his body heat.
Focus is shifted to the water as it approached,
And as the ocean's madness is realized, its intensity screamed like a coach.

A vivid daydream is what he'll meet,
Just sit right there boy, hold that seat.

Sand sand luscious sand
Colored in a candied Persian silk persona.
The beatles mantra rings inside his head,
'Love is all you need', but what do you need when you are dead?

Twisted and turned and as confused as he may sometimes be,
He sings,
"The demons scratching at my feet, they will not reach,
I'll find me a goal,
A goal that makes sense and fits within my soul.
Narrow fountains and dense brush dance, filling my tender mind.
Come lay witness to the esoteric secrets that I may find."

Hush puppy hush, that bark is in need of a shush.
Surrender to the waves as they come,
They cannot take you, as you've become overgrown and lush,

he finally finds his logical blindness that's parked behind his chest.
He consciously embraces the water as somewhere to peacefully rest.

Do you? ⸰

7/8/21

Do you still get scared of the dark?
When in water, do you think there's a shark?
When the demons come out to play,
Are you one who shies away, or
Do you fight them and face the day?
When the demons come out to play.

Are we made to be afraid?
We will eventually fade.
We will be played and portrayed in a shade of gray unfit for us to masquerade.
When will it all end?
When is the end?
When exactly is it we bend down to commend our pretend friend formally named the end?

You see,
I think it's safe to say.
That when the demons come out to play,
I don't shy away—
I toss the ball.

Demon ‸

5/30/21

A demon is a repressed urge.

when I indulge ⁄

4/6/23

There are days I lean into oblivion—
There are tears to be tasted with a glass of fine wine.
And a play with a choir, which will be silent the entire time.
For if noise is made, it shakes the sand in the line.
I think the line's ambiguity is somewhat of a sign...

Dream me a dream of a lilac field,
Sing me a song filled with nude appeal.
There are warm bellied kisses to heal your patchy soul,
There's a star-studded mistress to make you feel whole.

Many books claim it's a sin,
But in death, you considered it a definite win,
Just lose your head, and when you're dead.
That is when, you'll wish you had read.

But hey after all you can hang in hell,
Shoot craps, drink gin, and play around with ms. mademoiselle.
You see, if you're a demented creature just as the one that speaks,
Then come and join the caravan of displaced freaks.

Tears stuck in time

11/27/22

The great sky has seen our smiles—
Forever locked in the natural order of this world.

What has happened, will never change,
These emotions we experienced sure did range.

Stuck in time, but not unlucky,
I cherish the real;
Moments fluttering by without warning.

One day the loss of each-other is something we may be mourning,
But the entire experience will shine.
A dime piece of the universe—
Unable to be changed, crystallized in time.

So, as I ask for another kiss—
Understand this kiss I will not miss,
As it's to be imprinted on life's history.
To the godless sky,
That to us, remains a mystery.

It's a beautiful sadness,
As it took something so wonderful to die,
to have a rose ocean of emotion—
come crashing in.
A violently spinning wind dial pointed towards salvation.

Although our time may be short or shorter, we are embedded in time.
We have a beautiful piece of representation.

...

Hello again dear,
I'll always have some love for you,
We're human.

Embrace the future, whatever it may be,
Write the present,
And come to peace with the past.
For, even temporary stories within the entropy of this world,
forever last.

This child, coerced by darkness ⸙

9/17/21

Don't be afraid, little one,
The dark cannot hurt you.
It will only coerce you.

Fear is something that this child never felt.
A child's mind is fragile.
It can be easily damaged,
Like an eggshell or a snowflake.

A child's mind is like a blossoming rose,
Just flowing in the wind,
Collecting whatever it may come across.

This child saw death.
This child understood the end—
This is the first time this child tasted fear.

This child understood that red is blood,
This child felt heartbreak.
This child understood the affliction of fire—
This child felt the discomfort of night.

Too smart to be ignorant,
This child saw the loss of god.
The heartbreak of neglect.

Who cared for this child?
With the illusion of childhood security broken,
This child grew quick.
This child knew to live is to suffer,
And that there aren't facts—
Only interpretations.

Damned the smart are,
Blessed are the ignorant.
Blessed the smart are,
Damned are the ignorant.

Ephemeral Symphony ⸓

8/21/21

The moon has glimmer, shimmer, is never dimmer than a lamp afar.
The moon tells us why,
Tells us why, we eventually need to die.
It comes in cycles,
Comes from nothing and grows into a full creature.
Only to fade back to nothing.

Life makes illustrations of us all,
And then death delivers a recall.
A recall into the darkness from which you've came.
Then for a time on Earth people will remember your name.

But eventually everything turns to dust.
Understanding the transient nature of life is a must.
For when you face your time to die,
Embrace your physical experience, for it was what it was.
Allow your flesh suit to perish, as you're released with a sigh.
And accept time's continuity as it persists,
farewell, goodbye.

uncomfy, hold me ⸲

4/20/23

There was,
There was not,
There is,
There it goes.

No time to pretend 'that' is still yours.

You see,
Sometimes even something that possesses your passion can burn you,
Even when you give it the best effort you know how.

And when the iron that brands your soul falls,
Picking it up could only result in scabbed hands.
But if you let it go,
You've become open to hold again.
open to being held.

being held
being,
held.

Concessive growth ⸰

6/4/23

I'm scared, will somebody hold me?
I don't wanna hide from the monsters anymore.
They have always managed to keep their eyes visible to me.
I know they watch.

Sometimes I get smart and tune them out.
Although,
...I know they lurk.

These monsters, they have these wild grins, I wish you'd see it.
They keep whispering towards my cradle, I wish you'd hear it.
When it's late and I'm nodding off, their breaths hold me captive.
I hear their nails scratch drywall.

You see, a child can only learn so much from whispers until they are confused.
And the monsters knew this,
Which is why as this boy grew—
the monsters shifted to more dialectic persuasive tones.

Old enough to begin thinking for himself, still playing with toys.
This child zips skin to flesh as morning ritual,
In order to suit up.
The monsters take note of his nude form, demented and disturbed,
That is why they make this boy feel comfort when he plays ball with them.
They have watched his life occur.

He doesn't feel alone, with the freaks.
While these monsters have taught this child a lot,
To him they were not glued.
He watched his life unfold as their deaths ensued.
Always wondering if they were really friends,
I suppose that depends on if this boy transcends.

They taught him darkness and that's a lot.
I suppose it's something that can't be bought.
I guess he now knows how monstrous skulls rot...

When pure evil comes to taint a soul,
Whether this child breaks is only somewhat within their control.
Limping from evil, he now understands,
Stuck in limbo darkness is what these creatures demand.
Attached, he'd never feel whole.

And he won't be able to break from his chains,
Until he realizes since birth he'd been tricked by demonic console.

Disquiets solace -

5/27/23

I exit my tent and find a well-stoked fire cackling in the delicious rain,
I find myself laughing.
With no one awake, memories of campfire cheer flood my mind—
Smiles, joy, and experience.
Yet— you'll find an incessant worm clawing at my brain.

As I lazily float on my back in water, with not a maelstrom in mind,
silent humming roars of a nearby waterfall offer solace,
In forgetting the haunting bellows that ring in my head.

As I walk through an illuminated park,
Foliage surrounds me, trees scraping the night sky.
—I cannot help but hear a persistent scream.

As I fall into the sweet cradle of a drowsy daydream,
I hear voices that have passed and see faces that in my life had never last.
How interesting.

My attention is snapped back to my pungent reality as I sense sharp irritating projections.

Perhaps all this discomfort I experience in my unrelenting haunting is due to my own
internal disintegration.
My own insecurities, my ambiguities.

I've been tied to driftwood that finds itself fortunate enough to be roughed by the falls,
I've escaped the doll house and have found myself in the rumbling talls.
Leaving fond comfort to be thrown around in hopes of finding discovery, is quite the
bearing.
And whatever I may discover in my malaise, believe me I will be sharing.

Kujo ✦

4/4/23

Deathly beaten bread winner that sits alone and laughs,
Directly cheated business dinner that gets the man a deal.

Fight for your survival is the aim of his religion,
With devouring practices that eat morality, what does he have left?
The cold jeweled moon that yawns after he dies does not care that he won his simple game.
It cares that you won, cradling the youth of the young in the song that you sung.

.∴.

Dig yourself a womb that you shall finally rest in,
Visualize this final tomb—

—As your soul forms from gas.

'Did you leave a good world when you died?
Enough to hold a baby too?'

...

A callous potential is built through troubled youth,
A palace of good manners is built upon the backs of fathers with couth.
But what if the father was in lack?
Surely that wouldn't have justified this man's attack...

Freaka growl ⸏

7/16/23

Nevertheless, freak a growl.
Growl at freaks? I'm confused.

Leave freaks to growl?
Don't you howl.

hunny.

Ego play ⸗
11/29/21

I respond well to dead people,
My ego doesn't have anything to compete with.
Malicious ego will not carry you to where you want in life, I understand.
But day by day I keep catching my ego yearning to materialize as crisis on hand.

as I see with clear eyes, my reality fails to realize...
Ego can be enemy, ego can be tool,
Under masculine control, ego can be a jewel.
Help you work, help you dine,
Ego can bust you through times, you don't feel fine.

Death makes people your own?
Their life experience is perceived through your own lens.
They almost become a part of you.
If you ask your brain to have them give advice on your situation, their words will manifest.
I cannot become jealous of a dead man.

For that I must state,
most men that wish me the best,
have nothing residing inside of their chest.

Nuance of Evil ⸍

Clouds flow through mountain valleys like boiling rivers,
trust me your true self won't give me the shivers.

I think it's important to take people in as a whole,
accept that there have been times evil has taken its toll.

But to define someone strictly by their deeds,
is to trap a bird, and refuse it seeds.

When we can digest and balloon their intentions,
Their person cannot be tainted even when people do mention, evil.

I think it all resides in how a man laughs.
Can his belly belt and boil? Or does he calculate a snicker with toil.

Oh, to judge. I think that absolutes aren't to be stood on, but generalizations come with
intelligence, and anybody with a brain can make conclusions with accuracy.

I think you can know people fairly well based on the million and one cues they exhibit.
I'm not guessing, I'm making inferences as I live it.

...

True evil comes rare, people typically taste moments of evil's touch. But never too much.
Rotten apples are real on the other hand, as I've witnessed a few. Studied them, and
developed a sense of their hue.
These are humans who are born of sin, bred for greed and debauchery.

I've witnessed far too much to have a single bad move from a humane friend define them,

With my eyes.
having seen the strangest life I've known,
where evil's grown and dissolved. Bliss has roamed and tumbled.
I've seen a few of life's corners.

Judge with intellect.
And define with flexibility—
No one answer.
Shhh— Listen to the screams—

17 children of Satan ⁓
10/8/21

17 people await their trial,
Murder is what taints their name.

Now on file as juvenile monsters,
They will never get to see the handsome stars,
Never will they see the big bright dot in the sky that is Mars,
All because their rage boiled over and spilled.

Now consumed and wounded with regrets,
A heavy pitted feeling won't release from their chests.
They feel stuck, waterboarded by circumstance, unable to capture a full breath.
true panic

Each mother wishes they could look their child in the eyes and tell them not to fret, that it will all be alright...
But sadly, they cannot...
Burnt innocence, sinner, scum,
The only thing they felt they had left on Earth was their fathers' peachy bottle of piquant rum.
But this wasn't true.

It's supposed that it took rightfully declined freedom to realize what they actually had,
A soft mattress, clean water, and anxiously free faces.
There's an old saying that everyone and their dog knows,
"You don't know what you got until you lose it."

These people, kids, now know this better than anyone,
The wisdom hit them like a brick wall hits a sports car in the dead of night.

Untamed with passion

9/12/22

Damage is done,

flakeless flawless,
My brain yawns for forgiveness
Yet the damage is done.

What have I done–?
Did I find it fun? Because it makes me sick.

It pricks me, the discomfort tricks me—
Why did this behavior pick me?
Was I in control?

Help me find the war-like courage to proceed as morally planned...
Yes, this mistake of mine may have been caused by demonic distraction.
But it is a responsibility of my own to orchestrate the removal of any cancerous tumors
present on my soul;

Erroneous decisions have played their tune, resulting in—
Contention within my soul.
Driving me towards the removal of behaviors that rot my flesh—
This will be savior.

There has not been a single time I have felt right with these poor-hearted positions.
Sometime soon this darkness will fade, and my light heart will be played; to have itself
another repetition.

Because today I've decided—
What I do is
within my jurisdiction.

Shhh, the babies sleeping ‸

5/28/23

Where in the world will I rest?
Lay down my body.
Silence my mind.
Meet my maker.

As an explorer of profundity, I continuously face potent fears and assaults, fortunately I
turn them on their heads and help use them to keep tuned my realizations.

A diver of the depths will forever have a degree of solitude.
No matter how much company,
No matter how many lovers.

The deeper you swim,
The further you'll find yourself from the water's tension.
From the gaseous aura that supplies common life.
—Separated.

The further you stray from the sun, the external confounding light,
The darker internal depths you'll face...
The less populous...
The less light that can be seen.

The journey ends at the bottom,
Or so some think,
many who explore, die in the dark fluid abyss,
Straying from the light of ignorance in hopes of finding deeper truth.

Deeper truth they do find,
but this 'deeper truth' on the ocean's floor engulfs their soul in gloom.
They find their final bed in darkness.
As bones do not float.
The more layers of flesh they seemingly shed,
The more the weight above seemingly squished and hurt.

Now... for a handful of individuals somewhat alike— They arrive at the seabed and refuse
to accept perpetual darkness.
—Looking around, they see gravestones,

With epitaphs written, "Truth lies, it does not float."
Is this truth? Indefinite darkness–?
These special bunch of divers may linger for moments longer,
But soon.
They begin to dig deeper—
Excavating untouched stone— miles of boring.
Eventually after what feels like an eternity, given the unrelenting desire for truth,
the abyss begins to turn molten little by little,
Giving tastes of the light but still,
shrouded by darkness.

That is of course until,
The final barrier is broken,
A bright boiling ball of heat is what they'll meet,
They've reached the core.
They may rest in peace and self-actualize.

...

If you stare at the abyss long enough, dig deep enough, you'll find yourself, something ever
brighter than the vacuum of ignorance that is the surface.
Explore
Truth.

A blurry chronicle ‑

Oceans of white paint coated sane lies.
A bright island surrounded by water filled with sharp questions.
Trying to navigate through this rocky jungle of liquid can leave scars on your feet, a hidden branding.
This liquid is not clear; it's thick, colored with white, outstanding.
To escape this island seems impossible, for the true depths lack clarity, it is too opaque.
You could get quite cut up in an attempt to escape.

Truths voluptuous color, never to be touched,
Authenticity is clouded, as you've sailed yourself to the island as such.
and
to call for help means—
trust is broken.

I was a weak man once in another life, where my told story was apocryphal,
and before that life I was a weaker man.
The time passages that have led me towards salvation, have been filled with trials and exaggerated dissonance.
Tending to get stuck in poor mindsets when my attempts to control reality fail.
There are many vicious soul sucking self-pity fueled false indoctrinations that we consume,
we never get the clear picture, only the liquified truth.

I shall rise; my sails. Traverse above my lies,
and finally, shall I be surrounded by reflective shine.
New horizon revealing what's truly mine.
Patience and gratitude, a yearning for truth,
I
am
Modified and shall set sail, above my false youth.

Bitter? No. ⸝

12/31/22

Bitter?
I try not to be, haha...

Fleeting delight ⸱

2/19/23

A needle that finds its freedom, is'n vain,
Skull-shattering kisses sane men contain.
Doping embodies— false womb; now afloat,
A mother that never smiled, sunken boat.
Union born of blood, tied spirits forget,
Broken down and hungry for love, regret.
Sought release, results in scraped knees,
Mud-puddled tears; the love pale and dying.
Gone and put away; the thought remains.
Would its return relieve, or would they leave?
Pretend now, for the time is over, they're gone.

... ´

2/12/22

time to go brag about ego death...

Embers of Liberation

5/24/23

Bathing in an opulent smoked scent—
My home is burning down.
As I sit and watch, I don't even squeak a sound.

I watch from the hill across the way,
An earthly bump I roamed as a toddler.
If you look into my reflective eyes,
You'd see my cold eyes' glaze filled with the image of wildfire ravaging inside of my room.

So many things I assume I need.
—But this pungent blaze's truth is now my gift,
For now... I'm finally freed.

No more things to tie me down.
I can easily skip this now old town.
Burnt to crisp are mementos,
satin pillows, and even my old scrap manifesto.

The cottons weight won't hold me down,
For I've been born again from its roaring sound.
The fire is hot or so I'm told,
but maybe for me it'll just be cold...
Reject the lie that I've been sold.
'I need these things that I can hold.'

...

Now that I'm above egos deceptive lies,
I can rid these heavy earthly ties.
Move somewhere new and start afresh,
All I need is my effervescent flesh.

Wood smoke ⸌

12/30/21

If my home happens to burn, I will find sanctum in acting dumb.
The fact that I will not cry aloud does not mean I am numb,
The fire's at my lawn, yet no emotion, not even a crumb.

Our reality is inherently chaotic, so I've decided to embrace.
If fears preachers come to chase me... I will not race.

There is no point in running from these fires—
For... a life scared...
is a life that tires.

Embrace disorder, chaos, and all alike.
For it comes coupled with strength,
That is of course, if you learn to harness life's pain, in length.

This passing chapter ⸜

6/18/23

As the wind catches my sail,
I'm pushed away from a chapter.
Towards refreshing experience.
Lessons learned, people tasted,
That time has concluded in being created.

Memories flush my eyes as I stare at turbulent sea ahead,
I know that given my best effort I will not wash ashore dead.
The true challenge will be in keeping a level head.

So much experience encapsulated in a single chapter.
The baby bird left the nest,
Pain was an opportunity; pain was a test.
Growth can occur without witness,
although, focused effort is fertilizer.

I fell at the knees of my sin,
My neediness, my indulgence,
Fear.
Gruelled in insecurities,
Knew nothing about my place in the world.
Fell in love.
Fell out of love.

Pain spawned a fruited bird's song,
which began to thrive in hell.

As I built my boat plank by plank, I prepared myself to set sail.
I understand the weather will wail,
And perhaps I may sink.
But when it comes to my brink,
When death comes a-knockin'.
It is only then that, I shall rethink,
my reality, independently, decide.
Allow myself to drown.
My fears dissolve,
My sins absolve.

This upcoming frontier,
Unknown mountains,
Jungles to be crossed.
Dear mother earth,
I will do my best.
Dear my younger one,
observe this here test.

You, Reader.
You're worth more than you think.
Keep pushing towards your promise land.

Take my hand my dear,
Close your eyes,
Embrace uncertainty.
Repeat after me,
'When I'm hurt, I will stand,
Life is grand I demand,
To figure out my entire hand,'

A breathless cleanse ⸱

5/15/23

The sentiment that we must sometimes push ourselves rings true... Well?

If by sometimes, it means every time. I suppose "must" is a stretch, for you will not die—
But something greater shall pass, never come to fruition.
And that would be the phantom that dove,
The being that did, the one that had.

It was you.

It was something attainable,
But now the shallowness of one's will and the deficiency of one's comprehension have
assisted in its decomposition.

Every day we wake with a choice,
Every moment we are faced with a voice. Clarity.

There is a question we must ask ourselves,
Are we really doing everything we can?
How important do we find it? Must we?

Count yourself,
How many pieces are there that ring far too scatterable?
How much electricity escapes? Are you accounted for?

When we can understand that the pain of never having lived to digest the scope of our
furthest push
has more mental weight than a concrete mattress,
Our potential can materialize.

Once done, there is no question of the alternative's validity.
You have no other choice.

The pain may float above to sink you like a glass plane in rocky water,
But the feeling of needing to breathe is a false reality ever capturing your fate.

Allow yourself to drown.

The cold wash shall soon begin to burn,
Digits will dissolve first,
Thought will dissolve last.
Day after day of endeavor
A great future will be built, brick by brick, stacked by your past.

All you must ask yourself,
Is "Will I capture it? or will it have passed—"

Death the beauty ✦

12/12/22

Surrounding me like a rapid in a river,
Death the beauty surrounds me in life she makes me quiver.
Just one false strife and she's realized,
You will never forget her teal eyes.

Death the pretend friend?
This was falsehood I had embodied.
Now as the blades edge slits my throat,
And thick blood covers my coat,
I remember the drowsy daydreams of my childhood.
I surrender to my mousetrap.

Serrated clouds creep my memory,
Uneasy thinking stashed beneath gives room for conversation.

Til' tomorrow I was in my cotton-brained infancy.
Death the beauty fears nothing, she accepts all human resistance.
Pretend friend? I'm unsure about that, but certainly death cannot be your enemy. She is an anti-enemy.
I've found a new love for myself, serenaded myself to my highest degree,
So far,
I've learned, no war leads to leakage.

Spiced demons with stone colored flesh race my mind during evening.
Gorgeous moss covers my soul like a rash,
As I race towards endless salvation I dash;
For I missed the starting gun.

The corner cottage within my mind collaborated with my essence to realize the terms of my catastrophe,
I will get nowhere without true unrelenting effort.

Sometimes I forget why I tick.
Then I remember my heartbeat—
Even in the moments I cannot hear my internal thud,
I shall not stay complacent sitting in mud.

Death the beauty does she have a heartbeat?

Strung in silk with skin as smooth as milk—
Dark resilience and mystic experience,
Death provides beat hearts a final retreat.

I must stay nimble, I must keep on my feet,
For as conclusions are thrown,
I've grown to follow desires that my soul has shown.

Death the beauty has no rest—
Death the beauty an inescapable test—

I know how to hold my hand to fire,
The smell of my flesh melting is something that doesn't tire.
The true lesson I capture from the fumes of pain:

'Embodied gratitude and acceptance
Makes me feel whole.'

Freedom

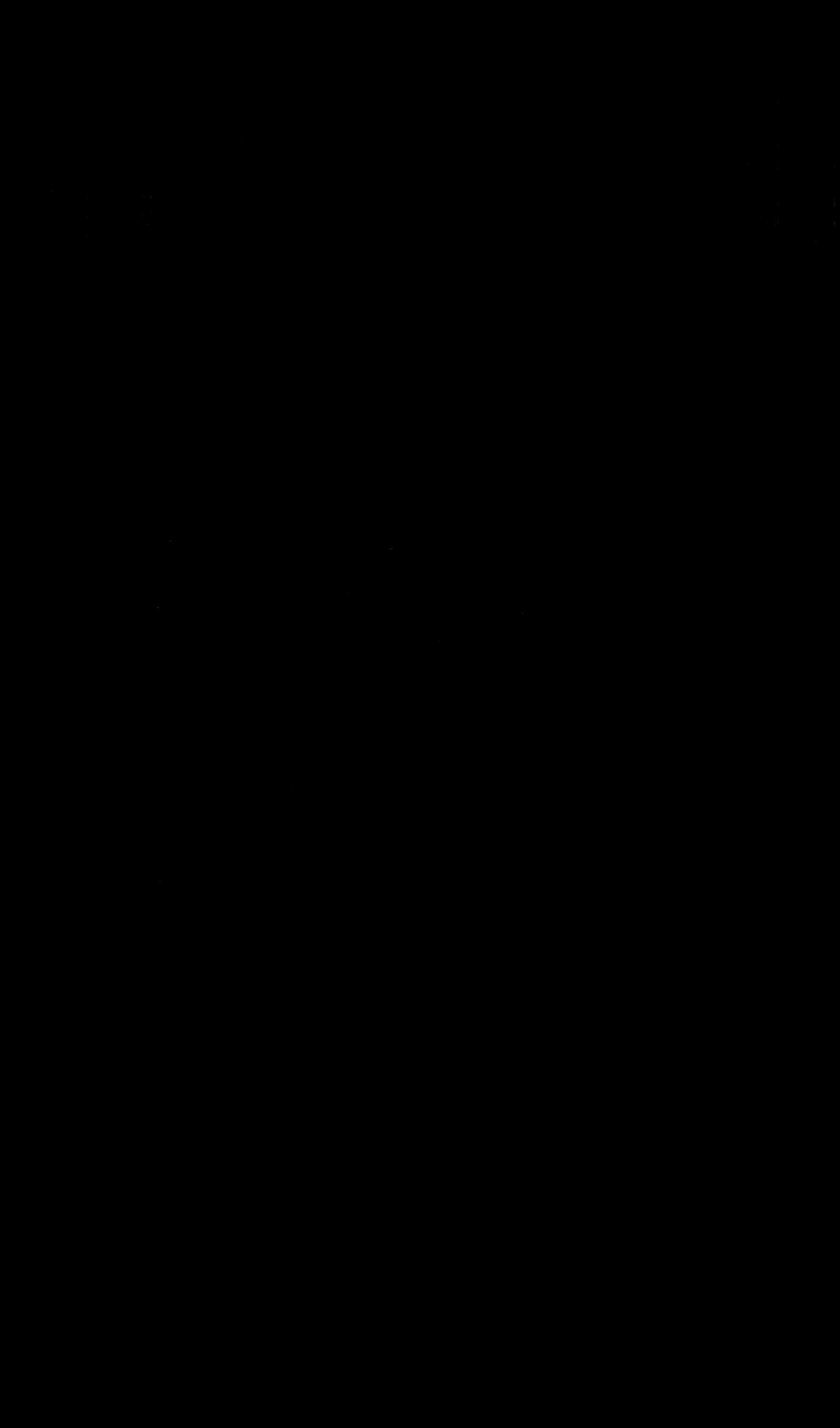

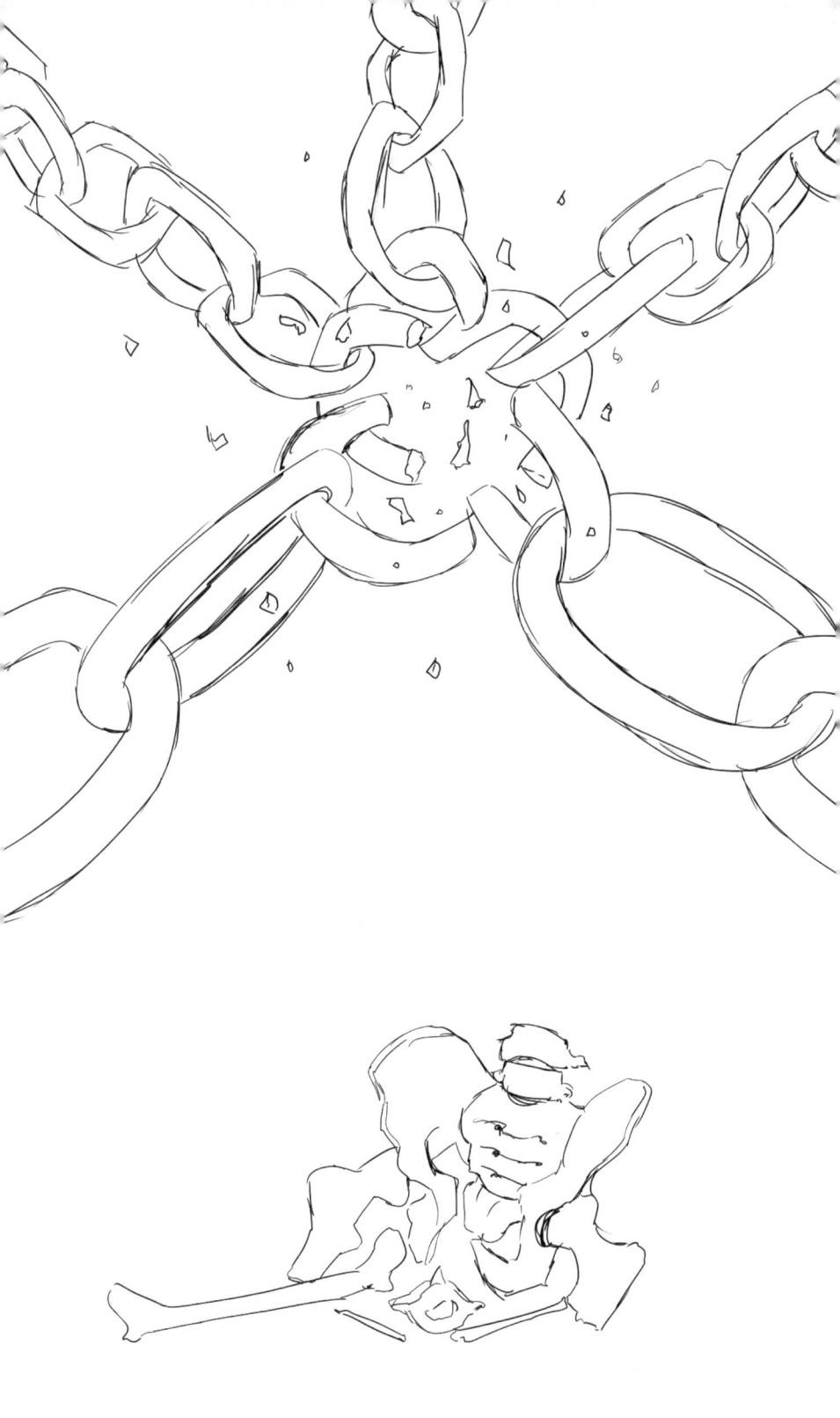

Sweet swinging freedom ✐

1/4/23

Sweet freedom lingers on the tongue of the buried.
'Hush now ambitious child, this lifestyle cannot be hurried.
Just put your head down and work,
Work beyond the capabilities you've assigned yourself to.
Work towards freedom.
Don't you know you're perfectly in control of your destiny?'
Listen now,
Sometimes I have to threaten me,

'Life will be miserable if you don't step up to the plate'.

A 9-5 my child is something that you will hate.
Find a way to build freedom or you'll degenerate.

Life's witness could be so great.
Self-fulfill prophecies that self-create.
Occasionally you may be
consumed with vice and hollow. Remember
strength is built upon the fields, worked with tools of sorrow.
Your willpower cannot be killed if you don't allow it.
Some demons may try to borrow it. But
in the end, don't play pretend,
stand your ground,
and create authentic self.

Authenticity's effort you see, but pays excellently.
Be a friend to the tasks that care.
And when you ask for strength and life sets its snares—
Test yourself, seeing how your idea of self fares.

Pray for the Eiffeler ✓

1/6/23

Trials and tribulations,
their deceptive portrayals meant to disturb my foundations.

My beliefs, my creation? met with derision.
Driven by spite, they work to blur my vision.

But let me share this with you, my friend,
I have been led astray; I do comprehend.

Now, every hardship that comes my way on my attempt to return,
will teach crucial lessons that I was always meant to learn.

These adversities, though hard to bear,
Have guided me towards salient life lessons, to which I've been made aware.

And as a result, from this big ol' shebang.
I've grown stronger and shall keep my eyes fixated on the key to my shackle and chain.

Angelic Chords ∕

3/22/23

With the death of a cradled star,
A new vacuum within the chasm of space reveals.

Fill it with grace, discipline, and discovery.

Without heaving distractions your mind will ring,
But now more than ever it's important to sing.

Floating dreams into purposeful life ⸜

6/15/23

I will not chase my dreams.
I will pursue my purpose.

Dreams are figments,
residing in their own quirky state of intangible limbo.

Change your diction.

Purpose becomes something you must do, because if you do not engage in your purpose,
Why are you living?
You are clearly capable,
And yet, you try so little sometimes.
It's not because it's hard, that you do not try—
It's hard, because you do not try. *Shoutout Seneca*

Stop at nothing but your life's dusk in pursuit of your defined dreams, your purpose.
You weave the reality you become.
So don't get lazy.

unlaced dreamkiller ✧

4/7/23

Hope was a dream,
Hope never would seem—
in touch—

—Until the sky fell and my skin flaked.
I was desultory, set in wet concrete.
Until I realized that wasn't true, wasn't opportune.

So much more to do,
idealized an existence of self.
Picked my poison from the shelf,
and fell into a vacant womb.

This womb still bubbles,
and my rebirth struggles.
But it shall triumph.
As it comes with effort,
and laces in my shoes.

No such thing as inevitable ⹀

1/21/23

I beg of you— reread your deed,
The deed to yourself.

Examine—
Personal accountability, ownership.

No one is coming to save you,
You are the only person responsible for your life,
Nothing is guaranteed in life—no degree of success, no special life path,
It is all created.

There is one thing inevitable, and her name is death,
Nothing more will be handed to you through fate itself.

If you want to live a grand life teeming with persuasion,
Ask yourself:
Do you rule your body? or do factors unseen, uncontrollable.
Do you sit tense, contracted, speaking in contradictions?
diction varying day by day?
Or are you dialed in, focused on desire–?

Change.

Perhaps it is understood, perhaps it's not.
No one and nothing is coming to rescue you from yourself.
Personal accountability, ownership.

Your life is your responsibility, and almost everything you get out of it,
Or more importantly, everything you don't—
Is a tangible creation within control of
your own manifestation.

So many callings, ⸴

3/26/23

So many callings my ears ring,
Lost and confused yet my soul sings.
I know that wherever I may drift—
Graciousness and a lightness of being, coupled with kindness, is what will
fill my void.
Transcension from needless tension is— artistically formulaic.
hear me out—

—Fairy children that laughed without care
Now stand saddened by the death of a loved one—

Don't forget that life, regardless of circumstance,
can return to its bliss and contentment,
so long as you reinforce positivity within yourself.

Don't give up on a smile.
Don't give up on brightness.

Sometimes to live is to suffer,
and the point of 'being' is to experience pain.

Just know that no matter what you think,
You're worth more than you believe.

Sometimes you'll get ruthlessly hard on yourself.
It's times like these, which require great self-care—

Forge your thoughts into goals,
and then take steps to achieve such roles.

Given your effort towards that formula,
mixed with a little self-love,
watch as your life becomes prosperous once more.

If you fall off the wagon— it's okay.

Rinse and repeat—
These kinds of things can be cyclical in nature.

Goodluck.

Panacea

6/12/23

Are you worthy of freedom?

B.O.P.

7/27/23

Bird of prey

Flying high—
In the sky.

Go-
ing for a ride.

Floating on
Invisibility.

Searching for
it's prey.

—fleeing birds,
Catching wind.
Little ones.
Scared of death.
Running for their
—lives.

Hidden among us ✦

6/26/23

If you claim to always know,
You'll never grow.
Like a weed I'm unsettled,
sprouting between a rock and a hard place,
Yet I find my sunlight.

I know I know I know,
I fear to grow too big because I may be plucked;
Uprooted with my intentions miscomputed.
A weed has no malice behind its growth,
It's simply the design that we loathe.

Do we truly get to state what beauty is?
And what rejects should die?
Sure, some's functions are as annoying as those of flies.
But that does not mean they are, bad guys...

A stinging nettle can help a butterfly bush to thrive.
Dandelions will make for food in a bee's hive.

Perhaps we know and perhaps we don't,
Beauty is in the mind of the beholder.
Don't play fool and count out the ugly, the bad.
For perhaps its erasure will make the sky sad,
As we failed to realize the subjects that we had.

Liberate the Verities ⸜

6/8/23

The aberration of shifting perspective is potent: "Wow, I now know! Wait? I don't know. Wait, how do I know? Okay what's known? What do I know I know? Was that true? Oh dear, my life's a lie…"

So many people are stuck in what they're told to do, because they've been told they have to —and they see no other path that's true.
There are so many lies that sing the sheep to sleep and convince them of what they must do.
Yet some are resistant and don't cower to deceit.
Question everything you're told to believe and stand sturdy on your own two feet.
Question your beliefs and figure out their origins.
You're being tricked if you believe you must live a life you hate.

Go to the mirror and command yourself to orate!
"It is possible through hard work and determination! It is possible through hard work and determination! It is possible through hard work and determination!"
Caress your dream and make it yours,
Ambition at any age can open doors.

Take a look inside your mind, remove false gunk that you may find.
Remember,
You're indomitable and capable of all,
Your situation is at your own beck and call.
Make a plan.

Reject limitations that lead dreams to waste,
And stray from the complacency in which you've been placed.

Race for freedom, lay down your hand.
You can live on your own terms and be free—
you must understand, you create the person you're destined to be.

What I think about, suffering, ⸰

7/22/23

I think that— the times
I've hurt the most,

Have been the times I've grown the most.
Have been the times I've learned the most.
Have been the times I've discovered the most,
About myself.

...

It definitely does not feel good when your world is in disorder,
And you believe your situation to be unfixable. undesirable.
The food becomes bland,
And you feel displeased with your experience,
Because life didn't pan out the way that you had planned.

Misery can consume some people whole,
becoming their drug.
Infecting their bloodline.

The power of Misery, the power of Grievance, the power of Death,
Each live free rein within 'the miserable man',
Bending him to his wits.

The individual who grows on the other hand, 'the growing man', uses
all three clusters of energy, In order to
fuel their own personal developmental hell.

Self-reflection becomes self-redirection.

Channeling these potent energies into personal development and self-understanding,
This is how 'the miserable man' converts into 'the changed man'.

There's this idea that has always helped me personally.

The simple fact that, within some periods of your life,

your highest purpose, the highest demand of you,
Will be to suffer.

True suffering,
grievance, loss,
self-hate,
discomfort.

Provides you with the opportunity to have access to a reserve of potent emotional energy,
Transitional in nature.
If utilized in the right way, this energy can change 'the miserable man' into 'the person he wants to be'.
It has the capability, to positively, redirect a life,
permanently.

Remember,
as you traverse through time's elaborate play,
Where you'll play witness to your own.
Keep in mind this here tip,
'If and when you receive an energy cluster that's presented as suffering,
Redirect it towards your own personal shortcomings that do need restructuring.'

The memo ⌐

11/21/21

Oh? you ain't got the memo?
The new one:
intuitive awareness discovered it.
Crying can free you from burden,
Shaking the trauma away.

It's a form of release.
And I'm not saying you should nor must forfeit your tears.
But.
Figure out and derive an explanation as to why crying could save you years,
"Symptoms of repressive coping." google.

Now I'm not saying sit around and feel bad for oneself,
But surely do not allow emotions to not be processed and stored on a shelf.
If you repress negative emotions and do not allow them to be felt,
they do not leave, instead, they form an internal welt. "Ouchie that belt!"
And believe me once they find a home, they are not good neighbors.

Even if it's not crying that you allow yourself, allow your body to find its own way to
mend, allow space for intuitive healing to attend.

Even if something may seem unrealistic, it could be as real as your thoughts beneath a hat,
don't be fooled by what your body does to mend its soul.
Crying, sighing, and all alike.
Don't allow your inner world to form a crystalized turmoil spike.

It's no secret the soul can fight it, bite it, scratch, and kill,
So, the soul must learn to release its will.
Allow the mind's attempted efforts within your brain,
forfeit the stalemate, or you'll remain the same.

That's it, Surrender, or else you may go on another angst bender!

Now. What's your modern definition of the word trauma?
I think,

it refers to any event or thing that haunts you, torments you in your mind.

Where did your trauma come from? Let's look and find exactly where.
It must be memory you don't even know is there!

Well,
What if it's not? Maybe you were just born with a little ounce of dark and twist
embedded in your genetics.
Not everything has a direct explanation, sometimes things just exist.

Do my thoughts exist?
Now that is a thought that I cannot resist.
Even if I tried to digest it fully, this thought will always persist.
I know this bottle exists, this shoe. This cup full of glitter.
Look here, I can even hold this old slipper.
I can feel it's weight! Surely this cannot be much of a debate. it exists. Or does it?

Thoughts however,
thoughts are the painters,
As things are the muse.

Can something metaphysical be real?
A thought exists, in the timeline of the universe.

"Matter cannot be created nor destroyed!
There's a finite amount of matter in our universe!"

Well, do my thoughts matter?
Are they matter, do they exist?
Thoughts have unaccounted-for timestamps.
If each one was captured and the data was collected,
It would exist.
Although, you cannot capture them in their nude form.

So, I ask you again, does the pile of stone in your head exist? Can it exist if not physical?
It is what it is, a constructed abstraction.

Ask me to prove something's existence, I cannot.
But when it comes to a thought of mine, I've seen it, experienced its sight,
So, to the question of, "does it exist?" I'd have to answer, "it might."

Examine this conscious entity that is you,
clearly it exists, but clearly it isn't physical.

imagine a castle,
Walk through its halls, be enchanted by all the paintings that are hung on its walls, did this exist?
Well, in its own form it did.

But what does that mean for what we know? Things exist beyond what we could ever show.
Everything is unknown? We are gods in our own right?
There is more than the physical realm.
There is love beyond love?

Once again for clarity. Our life, even in the darkness, has been gifted to us,
Nothing and everything is a rarity.

What's the moral of this tale?
Well, I'd say that occasionally you may wail,
For these thoughts and emotions that we experience,
Could perhaps pool and collect,
And could cause problems, if not checked.

And even though they are an intangible mess,
They still hold a sense of existence.

Allow your mind to heal itself.
There're real methods to heal that come from trust in oneself,
Trust yourself and you'll be left with better self,
I promise...

What's the deal with diamonds?

12/28/22

Strength is built upon fields of silver's gleam.
But, why silver? When gold may seem the ultimate dream?
It was close enough to touch, you've a fleeting hold,
As days pass and distance is covered, your dream of silver grows old.

Yet, perhaps it was destined to unfold this way,
As you've currently not got diamonds to display.
While you grow and evolve through trials faced,
Pressure shall transform your coal into refined grace.

Strength is built upon rivers of pain,
Mental paths altered, never the same,
Each day, striving with unwavering zest,
Sanity can be found in giving your absolute very best.

Progression and determination pave the way,
Unlike precious stones, resilience will stay,
With every hurdle overcome and position gained,
The brilliance of strength shall be ever sustained.

Caged rebellion ⸌

5/22/23

New age gunfire that attacks your soul comes from every angle.
—Our past's naturalistic ambient environment
has been replaced with a constant unrelenting hum.
...There is no choice.

You're born into it in this day and age.
It's like a tight cage surrounded by mirrors,
You can see the trap's nuances but
there's no apparent way to spin the code lock.

You're bombarded with advertisements and instruction on how to think.
A plastic aesthetic lines the room...
Nothing is handmade.

Alongside so much noise, there is always a constant drum of music—
...and it's not the kind that enlightens.

Stimulation is ever present—
Those who seek the freedom of silence,
shrivel to die.

In this anti-wild world, there is an escape.
Peel your skin to its nude undergarments—

You'll find that... as the flesh slimes,
and the tissue flakes,
Pain is nothing more than a signal.

Detach from your body to completely control it, and from this point of reason,
embrace that the only frontier away from a relentlessly stimulating outer-world—
are the gardens of your inner landscape.

Tranquilitas ✓

1/22/23

The gorgeous lilies and lilacs present as I walk along a still pond capture me.
Dazzling water with lime-colored pads is something I've found to lubricate my stuck mind.
Something quixotic, as its complex simplicity frees me from sub worldly obligations.

Sometimes we can get trapped in our thoughts and become ignorant to the radiant bliss
our surrounding world possesses.
This isn't our fault. In fact, it's human nature to create a dramatically cluttered inner
world consumed with turmoil,
This trend is plainly part of our instinctive corporeal quintessence. The human experience.

That being said,
Remember and reaffirm that—
It is our responsibility to ourselves and others to make effort towards a resolution of our
distaste.
Go produce an internal bloom.

Solivagant Serendipity ✧

6/23/23

Some days, even as I sit lady productivity on my lap and try her a whirl,
I find myself stewing and not doing.
When this happens, through lessons of my past, I find myself consciously caught before I clot.
"Clearly you're in need of new scenery my child".

Go on,
Set out for whatever adventure your intuition leads you to,
it's what you must do.

If that means walking down a few blocks to find a man strangling another,
Or climbing a new hill in which you'd find a hippie ready to call you "Brother".
North, West, South or East, find something new.

Expand your experience pool,
And your pool of experience will expand you.

Next thing you know, in an hour or two...
When you return to the steel seat of discipline.
With your day's exploratory fulfillment, that disquieting intrinsic itch, now fulfilled.

New scents will guide you towards undigested prosperity.
Fresh streams of conscious dialogue—

...

In times of stubborn thought,
Exit your comfort zone,
find new experiences,
Or else you'll rot.

blurbidy blurb ⸺

8/2/22

Sometimes the same residue will renew and happen to cause you to pursue the debut of a
brand-new view that will change the world and will change you.

Do you know that truth exists within lies?
That wicked souls are meant to play their roles.
Causal tides shift our worlds like beaches churn sand,
Something rough and rigid turned smooth and fashionable...

Which one of us will harbor the most lies?
Perhaps that is where our freedom cries...
Hidden in the fearful movement we give judgment and ego.

Inner freedom above social and moral posturing.
I've read somewhere that it can be acquired,
I suppose attempts to reprogram could be worth it.

What shall you get for all your effort,
Perhaps something bitter and tasteless,
Sharp and smooth,
Bloody and clean.

"I propose a new world where we calm down on the rampant egomania and social politics!"
Dammit... that was socially political and egotistically self-righteous...

Yes, a cost of internal innovation may be the invitation of envious malice.
But to create a wise world within... to work towards fostering a positive internal
experience...
It's the truest true that you can do... So why stop for— others...?

...And when it comes to the physical world you exist within,
Maneuver. Learn to maneuver. And do your best to influence your community positively.

Find your internal stability, built upon your truth,
Then cradle your world as you sip your county's vermouth.

Affixation: Let go and move on. ⌐

7/25/22

Capture and let it go...
For if back's the direction it shall flow,
to sew itself shut to you—
you'll then be more of a true mutt.

Ideas contort themselves to fit,
People distort themselves to get,
Steal, plunder, and take.

Be careful of what you allow to have sewn back,
For the people and things that sometimes return,
Are in need of examination,
Remember, there's evil you must discern.

After its absence left you burnt,
If you're quick to take it back,
There are lessons you had not learnt.

Then again... If you do—
Fail the test and misconstrue.
That's okay,
don't get blue—

For whatever happened isn't forever stuck like glue.
—A concrete truth that's yet to hit you.

Once reflected to your utmost capability.
you shouldn't think that anything should've been done differently,
because... it was what it was.

Hindsight is great,
although, it lacks realism,
What it felt like to be in the room—

Leave room for acceptance,
And learn your lessons, for the future.
As life will always be testing.

Do yourself the favor, and
don't allow the attachments that
disturb your soul— to remain within your world.

Tangled influence ⸜

6/17/21

You see, tough times don't last,
But tough people last.
That is if you allow them to.
Don't make your future a sticky past.

You must seize control of your social circle.
Don't spend much time with people who drain your energy,
Don't spend much time with people who emotionally manipulate you.
Don't spend much time with people whose advice pushes you away from your dreams.
Don't spend much time with people who aren't supportive of your dreams.
Don't spend much time with people who habitually break promises.
Don't spend much time with people who keep you down.

If you're a dreamer, find dreamers.

If you lack the people you need,
Cast a line out for new people.
Think of the type of friends and people that you desire to have in your life,
Then picture what kind of person these people would seek to have as a friend.

Then work to become that type of person.

You'll just have to evolve.
Evolve into the loving, witty, and progressive—
Person you can be.
This could make you much more... free...

You have to take the wheel,
Must assume control,
That's all that you can do.

A wise man once said something along the lines of
Before you diagnose yourself with depression, anxiety, et cetera,
Make sure you're not surrounded by a corrosive social bubble first.
It's not...
Easy to change,
But to achieve the dream,
Progress.

Friend ⸃

A friend is someone who allows you to be yourself, without judgment or inhibition.

Wise sales advice from pops ╱

7/16/23

The best piece of advice that my father has given to me today is as follows:

When you're selling anything to anyone and you've successfully convinced them, it's
important to know when to stop.
Once you've got them sold—
It's best to shut up.

Continuing to push or persuade someone who's already bought into your idea—
Just opens the door for them to lose interest.

This principle can be applied to other situations as well,
Such as if you need favors or others attention.
Once they've agreed to participate in what you desire, do not over-convince them.
Show respect for their decision.
Refrain from insulting their intelligence by assuming that they need more persuasion.

Remember,
People may become suspicious or uncomfortable if you keep selling them something that
they've already bought into. Even when if it's done out of love...

Attention ✓

7/23/23

When someone deems you valuable as a result of your charitable attention.
If you wish to remain—
Do not devalue your presence, by being overly present.

Resilience -

6/17/23

Throughout your life you will face disapproval and discouragement,
So.
Discouragement is what you shall conquer.

Each naysaying environment you're placed in will certainly challenge you.
But it is a responsibility of your own to rise above the negativity and doubt within any situation,
In order to create the life that you desire...

Remember,
Self-belief and a concealed hand is deadly.
Especially within an environment in which there are sharks waiting to pounce on weakness like blood in the water.

Don't give power to victimhood and manufactured capped ceilings, it will do no good for you. Battle and resist.
Understand that fear and judgment only occur because the source from which they are produced are afraid and judgmental of themselves.

Embrace your freedom.
allow the distractions no matter how many, and how potent to simply wash away—
Keeping your eyes fixated on raw desire to pursue what you love.

Discipline is even more difficult when you have an environment saying you cannot.
But it's in times such as those that,
Rising above your feelings and staying disciplined becomes of utmost importance.

You won't become what you can become if you don't put the work in.

If you want to become and do something great with your life,
It is your responsibility to yourself to take the wheel,
And steer it right.
And what does that look like? That is for you to figure out, through effort.

If your life ends up a complete failure, it is your fault.
If your life contains abundance of any kind, it was your doing.
You're not a victim.
No matter how dreadful your situation,

It is your responsibility to yourself to rise above it and conquer your day-to-day experience, which in turn will create movement towards success and fulfillment.

Being a victim is a useless cop out,
Your situation is of your own creation.

If you're unhappy, that is your fault and responsibility to fix.
Purpose will not be handed to you on a silver platter,
You're in control.
The answer to almost every problem is to work harder and endure the right pains.
It is possible, whatever 'it' is.
Push.

7/19/23
This does not mean that circumstance does not take its toll,
But believe me my friend there's so much within your control.

Resilient belief in oneself ⸌

7/1/23

Sometimes no matter how hard you try to show someone your picture,
They cannot and will not understand.

You could treat yourself as a windup toy and spin 'round discontent,
But trust me, that would do nothing but leave an internal dent.
So, calm my friend.

You may say exactly how you feel today, in perfect English, and they may display their
perfect misinterpretation.
You can show them your true message and they could get caught on each word.

Some people refuse to listen.
Some people won't change their minds.
Some people believe they know how you should spend your time.

Some people think they know what's best for you,
some people do...

But when you have a burning desire to push towards what you believe is right,
And people try to convince you that you're wrong.
Don't spend your time trying to persuade the naysayers and those who don't understand
your vision's worth.

Be true to yourself and don't get stuck on the fact that many people will never see your
side of the story.
Be true to yourself and don't get stuck on the fact that many people will never see your
meaning.

yelling yourself voiceless never helps.
Be authentic to yourself and embrace misinterpretations,

You may never be understood, but the least you can do, is,
be there for yourself to support and trust your own judgments and ideas—
you are powerful in your own right.

If you listen to your heart.
You will do what's best.
regardless of what others believe.

It's okay to be unappreciated,
It's okay to be misunderstood,
It's okay to be undervalued,
Do the right things,
and relentlessly follow your moral truth.

Be ‚

10/23/21

Be who you are—
and find people that appreciate that.

To reveal one's true self -

6/3/22

Like life, water will flow regardless of how the molecules feel.
Its pathed routes are strokes of the world's brush, a deep blue paint with specks of divinity
alive within.
Skin kissed by water is stripped free of its daily obligation to distort.

The pit in his chest subsides as water nips at the flesh
in which this unconscious vagrant resides.
Even in his own world, he sometimes hides.
Lies can be as cold as fluid.

To punish oneself for lies, one could walk on a trail captured by mineral spears,
Or soak oneself in the cold.
Perhaps that is not punishment;
For pain does have a silly little way of making him feel alive.

The hate we give,
the hate we receive.
Out here on this waterlogged-perimeter,
There is nothing we deceive.

I believe one day I will be open,
Just as the mountains' mouths that flow,
Maybe then
I will say that, "Today—

I repaired a part of me that was broken."
How'd it shatter? Well perhaps another day,
Perhaps then
I'd be willing to say.

Daoistic Investment ⸰

2/1/22

I've spent countless hours filling buckets to pour into the well,
I poured an innumerable amount of water into the fell.

I failed to realize that this hole is bottomless,
What was the cost of my vain effort to fill something unappeasable.
Was this idea I had unreasonable?

I believe that I should've taken a step back and had a deeper look,
Before I spent years trying to fill it with the thing, I only believed it took.
Oh well, that's life,
At least now I know,
I suppose this new information will
allow me to grow
in a way
I did not know.

Validate, necessary?

1/15/22

Must we have someone see our accomplishments?
our activities?
our life?
Do we truly need to satiate anyone but oneself,
I'm in a situation where...
Never mind, I don't feel like talking...

j

Evolution is my situations solution

1/1/23

Cold washed over me like a blanket,
But there I stood warm as ever—

The battle tried to tempt me towards death,
But there I stood smug and clever—

The abyss screamed to make me yearn,
But I wouldn't listen, not now, not never—

Ropes were tied to my feet and boulders were thrown to drown me,
but I took a deep breath and ropes I worked to sever.

Did I think I was meant to find salvation?
        I was unsure, I couldn't see three feet in-front of me.
But could I see my next step? Absolutely.
So that's what I'd take, make no mistake.
Regardless of my anxiety—

each step that is mine
helps me heal these wounds—
that apparently close with time.

I'm now doing better than ever. With a new year.
I suppose I've acquired closure— At least
Now I can understand exactly why I'm glad I kept composure.

You see,
Life will chew you and do you and screw you silly.
But at the end of the day, it's the price that you pay, for this great cosmic vacation that
is—this life underway.

For even when things do go stray,
evolve into something great.
Filled with love, not with hate.

Hold no bitterness nor resentment alike, you must truly understand.
No one is your enemy.

your reality is for you to accept; not for you to defend.

While some chapters you savored may come to close harsh,
Remember the wonderful, the bountiful, what taught you love, and what lessons you
learned from the marsh.
Wish nothing but the best for your counterparts that never were.
Remember the good, that's simply because, otherwise,
life would be   nothing   but   a   stir.

Patternized echoes on dash ⸝

5/11/23

Cold rain patterns my nude skin with echoes.
My bones freeze and crack. Facial grimace details the
mental meadows of which I travel.
My brain becoming evermore equipped for the torment of
worldly design.

Blood tasted.
Is never wasted.

Maturement,
endurement.

don't succumb to your 'cripple'.
run for solution.

Run like you need to catch your soul, not your breath.
For if this idea's embodied within your pursuit,
there shall be recapture
from death's stubborn absolute.

While everything's transience may still fill you with pain,
at least you won't be brittle, as
you dance through the rain.

...

Find the appetency to push beyond your perceived capability,
an expansion of capacity. Curing your
internal fragility.

Mindfully assemble—
agility.
Ready yourself,
seek out movement.

Proceed to find time to
wind yourself.

Cranking yourself up with
enough vitality to chatter towards the
table's edge, like a clockwork toy.
Once your chattering stops, at the edge of what's material,
circumstance will be—
your determining push.

From this edge will I fall
down into a bush?
A lake? Or perhaps, I'll land on
my all-encompassing toosh.

These possibilities, each and every,
seem to me, to be
uncomfortably real. While

Reality
on the other hand,
Possesses a degree of simplicity,
you see—

reality
is a production.
And you are
Executive.

Where will you spend eternity? ⏜
6/16/23

"Where will you spend eternity?"
The sign asked deliberately, religiously.

Well.
Me personally,
I believe I'll spend it captured in each moment experienced,
inscribed in time's keep-book.

That is where I will spend eternity.
Having existed moment to moment—
Each year tasted, each opportunity wasted.
I am impermanence seeking asylum in permanence.

Who knows better than miss majesty the future,
what will be seen next?
Inscribed for, eternity.

Now comprehending that our immortality resides in our fleeting sentience.
What will you do differently?
Grasp that, Every complaint and sour mood you possess
will have its own etching in your eternal residence.

Eudaimonia ⸱

6/17/23

The only way something can get on your nerves,
Is when you surrender your own control and energy over to it.

Whether you surrender your power or not, is within your control.
Sources of irritation are ideally to be observed, not digested.

There are a million things that should take away from your true bliss.
Such as⸱
A bickering person you cannot remove yourself from,
A broken piece of glass,
A lost wallet.
Or should they?

Are these incidental events what take away from your true bliss?
Or is it your lack of emotional competence.

It's very simple,
The concession of your emotional control and reactive choice is the one thing that removes
you from pure conscious content enjoyment.

Standing amongst rubble or standing amongst chandeliers.
You stand in space in which you can breathe.
It is how you perceive your environment that makes your environment; miserable, or,
beautiful.

Allow the trivial, the uncontrollable to flow away like a raindrop running off your nude
skin.

You alone have the power to choose how you feel, your attitude, your behavior, your
response.

Choose, bliss.

The way things are, ⸗

11/17/21

Instead of searching for a general meaning in things, search for your meaning.
Perhaps your life is leaning towards the perceived irregular.

Remember that caring what others may think will create a trap in which your
mental will sink.

Everyone was created by the universe to experience itself;
We are cosmic children.
So don't think small picture.

If you do not embrace your impermanence, the dreams you believe in will perish.
As compared to pass on.

Grieve for what you hold dear.
Lament because it lies six feet under, buried beneath cement;
No longer having to repent for these 'silly rules' that were godsent.

These rules were meant to control; well, is that a bad thing?

Is life really hard?
Or maybe it's hardly real?
Well, at least it's real enough to feel.

Life's a big deal, and greatness comes with hateless hats.
Because in a world of impermanence, how can hate be held wholly.

Bad Brains ⸻

1/22/23

"Bad brains,"
Said the devil.

I say,
"Harsh words, Mr. devil man—
At least I didn't lose a golden fiddle to a hillbilly down in Georgia..."

...

"The devil is the root of all evil! Everything evil is within his grasp!" or so they say...

Well... he used to be an angel.
Is he the root of evil? Or is he the angel that could identify with sin—
Or both?

...

While religious texts can have their fun, we must all ask ourselves,
"Who's the real enemy here, among us?"

Cowardice and self-righteous anger,
The snake in our heart, the lies on our tongues,
The arrogance of our intellect,
The gutlessness of our refusal to see.

The enemy is that which divides to sow discord.
The enemy is the pride and the fear that stops us from lending a hand across the divide,
The enemy is the eternal and great adversary of mankind.

Awakening from a hot nap ⸱

5/17/23

A dreadful catch within my stomach twists me whole,
this boil in my brain tells me, uncut, that something is wrong.

I question:
"What is this feeling and why do I feel it strong?"
I awaken to its origin.

"Ahh, I see..."
It's the comparative difference between my dreams and reality,
And it seems to be, making my ears ring red.
Not "...dreams" as in
I want to be successful in...
I want to get...
provide...
Achieve...

More so the taste of life,
The residue I have, to observe with open eyes, a hot daydream.

Within these subconscious states of deep exploration.
There's expansive wonder.

This expansive dreamish wonder that visits mind serves to contrast what occasionally feels
like a calculated reality. With brand names, and misguided moral positions—

Where are the cerulean striped sharks nipping at my feet? The holograms that dissolve into
my matter? The jungle with unseen heroes?

The childlike wonder that is abundance of creativity lingers strongly in my subconscious
and is where I work to go.
Great stories can take us there, but never to touch and never to keep.
The childhood beauty where you spent late nights, staying up, counting sheep.

To the people who value intimacy with the unknown:
"Our collective machine is under attack,"

You see,
There are many whom, decide to stand, at water's edge,

Leaping ledge, seems to them, to be a pledge, uncomfortable—
How serious a task, most will not last.
It's all because, complacency, complain you see.
C'mon, dare to be!
Jumpin' in!

Every night my eyes they close,
Reality magnifique is what I am shown.
Awakening back, into the cold... no wonder why, numbness gets old...
The adventure can, shift gears so quick,

"A baby made from stardust!".

Seek recapture from something bold—
Childlike wonder that speaks like gold.
I wish you all a sleepful rest,

See,
those dreams you'll see,
   they'll be the best.

Experimental fasting ⸌
7/18/23

The quicker I fall asleep,
The quicker I can eat pork chops for breakfast.

I've been hungry for days. Hunger is something without taste.
Thinking of turkeys that baste, and many delicious ice cream pastes.

I want a bite.

I am controlled—
So overwhelmingly controlled by these Earthly cravings—

Don't get me wrong I love food,
But currently I can't close my eyes without picturing carrots beings stewed.

Ohhh boy,
How I'm going to demolish the first chunk of meat that's on my plate.

I want— food.

I want something to nourish me whole,
Something to fill this empty bowl.
Perhaps a French roll,
Or some ravishing southern soul.

I suppose—
Although I am having drowsy wakeful dreams of creams.

—I am doing good nonetheless with all my doughy themes.

Desire ✐

7/7/23

You cannot have that cake, for greatness' sake.

Premeditated absurdism. ⸜

5/22/23

The mind can weave its way, joke to joke, to never conclude the laughter.
Hanging threads that appear can become fiber in an intricately woven get-up.
I suppose there's a reason they call it material...

...

While tragedies may be real,
Shouldn't one snicker at their loose threads?
For, they've been sewn.
Cannot be different. The past is behind.

If I pull from my intuition in search for answers,
I can acknowledge that,
Absurdism has rationale.

Help me to understand the absurdity of life.
The 'absurd' is something I feel I've known,
Yet have been unable to grasp...
As, I still take many things far too seriously.

...

Never not once have I felt entirely alone.
The cosmos are watching and laughing as I stub my toe.
It all goes to show that,
It doesn't matter if I wince.
Because, it's unimportance
adds a comedical bow.

"This is not a tragedy although it sounds bad.
I could laugh at anything!
Am I desensitized? Or am I just mad?"

I feel numb to the ruptures of my physical, I cannot feel my left foot.
Could I laugh at myself if I were missing limbs? as long as I could still lend a helping hand...
Some people at the edges of the most disturbed, can be found absurd. Living in a comedy.

Although I still have trouble grasping this concept, and would likely have a harder time with only one arm...

Believe me I am empathetic to all, but at the end of the day.
I know that laughing when you fall or get spat on is necessary.
There's no sensation in my foot...

Until recently, for me it wasn't understood that—
In walking
There will be pain,
but the suffering that comes with, is only a choice.
Also, I can't feel my foot... please help...

My foot......

A Metamorphosis ✔

3/19/23

Dreams thought to be rock-solid can become molten—
Heat that overwhelms, like salt in a baby's eye.

These forgone, far gone, now-gone days, that still hold grip.
Please, secure your seat for this roller coaster of a trip.

If you must, dip your sore paws into a new creek to wash dried blood.
Then do it.

You're occasionally meant to biblically be a fig tree. Cursed.
Some realities you believe you were never meant to see, were actually perfected reality.
Chasing peace will help you find hidden pain to conquer. Good.

Tear yourself and rebuild, just as a muscle's fiber rips to reattach stronger.
Strive towards brighter days but remember that it'll only come through persistent
disciplined suffering.

"I am me,
And I am to be,
Something that can set free,
causality, within what I'll see."

Face the sun alone and broken.
I'll tell you why—
Because the true will of the universe has spoken.

Expect nothing ✓
7/8/23

'To accept that you could die and rest alone,
To accept that you could never feel pleasure again,
To accept that nothing has to happen.'

When I meditate on this, it gives me a powerful piece of freedom.
A release from expectation. Expect and accept nothing.
And then everything will be a reward.
The sip of coffee in the morning,
The grass's sway.
The little moments that add up to the bigger day.
Pure Peace.

"Cherish each moment," I tell myself,
And through a method of self-hypnosis and repetition I notice I become happier.

I have not yet fully figured out happiness, haha,
But I am working on 'content'.
—there are certainly days in which I walk through limbo,
dreading the monsters that my ego produces.

But what I believe I have found fundamentally.
Is that discipline without expectation produces bliss.
So that is what I shall attempt and practice.

Keep an open mind, remain perspicacious ⌐

7/1/23

It's okay to change your mind, but don't blindly embrace others' convictions.
Stick true to your guns.

Only half the p... ⁄

7/23/23

If you never experience the struggle of rebirth,
You walk colorblind through life.

Deadly child ✗

3/23/23

Chubby cheek children, cheerfully smile,
They help to show me my lightness.
When I find myself stuck in the den of a stern situation,
The wonder within a child's eyes can return me to
acute presence.

I was a curious child too,
Eventually stung by indeliberate pain and subconscious lacerations.
For the good—

Wild child, screaming,
Dreaming of wilderness that quiets the mind...

this child seeming to be a gleaming
beam of hope,
destined to choke the life out of injustice and despair that surrounds.
That is of course only if this child could stop the choking.
A swollen throat that got tired of screaming,
completely sealed.

...

2012
Something's wrong.
Unease clouds the household,
This child was deadly.
Potent.
Potentially, a blessing.

...

2019
As he's grown a little smarter, he's convinced.
Only now he understands the influence that flesh can carry, or so he thinks.
Although still young, he carries himself well, or so he thinks.
Until his exploration of time continues, he shall remain in battle, a conquest of his own breath.

...

And in death,
He can only wish—
that he did his best.

•••• ⸌

7/14/23

Once again for clarity.
Our life, even in the darkness, has been gifted to us,
Nothing and everything is a rarity...

Devil's Highway ✦

5/5/21

Ride the devil's highway, baby.
Let's do it my way, lady—*fff*
—all the rules they made me.
Begin to go crazy.
My mind's on the fritz,
it's, becoming hazy,
My body's becoming lazy.
C'mon—
Let's share—
our crazy.

THE END

2021—

2022——

2023—

You've completed my first published poetic work!

I hope you enjoyed this book and now aspire to work towards a better-self— a purer soul of your own creation. As I know I am.

I appreciate your attention.

And I would love to hear what your thoughts are.
It would be very helpful if you left a review on this book.

If you think a friend would like this book!
Go right on ahead and tell 'em about this book.
We certainly don't need to gatekeep lady death do we...

In all seriousness,
Thank you for reading my book,
New work is coming soon, stay tuned.
You'd be doing me a great favor by suggesting my work.
And please share your experience with a review.

Until next time...

Hopefully I'll have grown out of my cotton-brained infancy...

Check out what I'm up to! -

YouTube: www.youtube.com/@CharlieArley

Instagram: **@CharlieArley**
X/Twitter: **@CharlieArleyArt**

Made in the USA
Thornton, CO
08/25/23 16:48:10

4de696ad-dd00-41fd-be76-174ae0a577bfR01